WADSWORTH PHILOSOPHERS SERIES

ON

R

en, Belgium

Australia • Canada • Mexico • Singapore • Spain • United Kingdom • United States

COPYRIGHT © 2004 Wadsworth,
a division of Thomson Learning, Inc.
Thomson Learning™ is a trademark
used herein under license.

ALL RIGHTS RESERVED. No part of
this work covered by the copyright
hereon, may be reproduced or used in
any form or by any means—graphic,
electronic, or mechanical, including,
but not limited to, photocopying,
recording, taping, Web distribution,
information networks, or information
storage and retrieval systems—without
the written permission of the publisher.

Printed in Canada
1 2 3 4 5 6 7 07 06 05 04 03

Printer: Transcontinental-Louiseville

ISBN: 0-534-60993-7

For more information about our
products, contact us at:
**Thomson Learning Academic
Resource Center
1-800-423-0563**

**For permission to use material from
this text, contact us by:
Phone: 1-800-730-2214
Fax: 1-800-731-2215
Web: www.thomsonrights.com**

Asia
Thomson Learning
5 Shenton Way #01-01
UIC Building
Singapore 068808

Australia/New Zealand
Thomson Learning
102 Dodds Street
Southbank, Victoria 3006
Australia

Canada
Nelson
1120 Birchmount Road
Toronto, Ontario M1K 5G4
Canada

Europe/Middle East/South Africa
Thomson Learning
High Holborn House
50-51 Bedford Row
London WC1R 4LR
United Kingdom

Latin America
Thomson Learning
Seneca, 53
Colonia Polanco
11560 Mexico D.F.
Mexico

Spain/Portugal
Paraninfo Thomson Learning
Calle/Magallanes, 25
28015 Madrid, Spain

to
Dirk van Dalen
on his 70th birthday

Table of Contents

    Preface

1. The Two Acts of Intuitionism   1
   - Ontology   5
   - Possible Cardinalities   7
   - Intuition   8
   - Truth   9
   - The Role of Language   11
   - The Place of Logic   13

2. Proofs and Logic   16

3. Choice Sequences   30

4. Brouwer's Proof of the Bar Theorem   40
   - The Theorem and Its Philosophical Interest   40
   - Brouwer's Proof   47
     - Part 1   48
     - Part 2   52
   - Some Comments on Brouwer's Proof   56
   - The Fan Theorem   59

5. "Creating Subject" Arguments   64

6. Intersubjectivity   72
   - Intuitionism and the Threat of Psychologism   73
   - Brouwer's Denial of Psychologism   74
   - The Creating Subject As Phenomenology's Transcendental Subject   76
   - Further Exploration   82

    Endnotes   85

    References   89

Preface

Luitzen Egbertus Jan Brouwer was born in Overschie, the Netherlands, in 1881; he formed a personal philosophy during his teens that would serve him all his life; applied it to revolutionize mathematics; founded modern topology on the side; and was run over by several cars in 1966.

'Although there is plenty of space on a gravestone to contain, bound in moss, the abridged version of a man's life, detail is always welcome,' Nabokov comments on his passage of which the above sentence is just a paraphrase.

The details that the following pages provide are meant as an introduction to Brouwer as a philosopher. This will be done by way of an introduction to his iconoclastic philosophy of mathematics, called 'intuitionism'. It is at most a minor exaggeration to say that the philosophical influence that Brouwer's ideas had, and have, stems solely from that part of his philosophy.

Specifically, I will give an interpretation of his philosophy of mathematics as he had developed it by the end of his life. The reason is not that Brouwer would have changed his view many times and one has to choose; one can, on the contrary, speak of the elaboration, over decades, of a single, complex idea, that of the creating subject. At the beginning, the notion of the creating subject was already present but mostly implicitly so; the development of Brouwer's intuitionism consisted in the unfolding of this notion. The unfolding did not proceed smoothly, for both the introduction of choice sequences and, later, of the creating subject arguments, were so rich in their consequences that they justify a division of the development of his philosophy of mathematics in three corresponding stages. It certainly testifies Brouwer's greatness as a philosopher that he came up with such original ideas in different periods of his life. During the development of his philosophy of mathematics, its various parts and the relations between them became clearer. Therefore, an introduction to this philosophy should benefit from concentrating at the final stage.

This particular approach to Brouwer as a philosopher has two consequences that I should mention.

First, the choice of approach has occasioned the sacrifice that several issues in Brouwer's thought, although of obvious philosophical interest, are not addressed as topics in their own right. Among these are his mysticism, his philosophy of natural language, and the applicability of intuitionistic mathematics to the natural sciences. I also have little to offer on Brouwer's eventful and complicated personal life. I am aware that this results in a certain distortion, and one should expect that in further study of Brouwer's philosophy these various aspects are drawn closer together again.

Second, on some topics in Brouwer's philosophy of mathematics I will dwell more determinedly than is done in other introductions to intuitionism, which no doubt have advantages of their own; I mention the continuity principle (ch.3) and the proof of the bar theorem (ch.4). The latter in particular may seem somewhat technical at first, and, though the chapter is self-contained, it may be skipped on a first reading; there is no question, however, but that of Brouwer's ideas, the bar theorem pairs the greatest mathematical fruitfulness to the greatest philosophical interest.

For discussion of the interpretation of Brouwer developed here, and for help in finding some of the sources, I am grateful to Jesper Carlström, Dirk van Dalen, Igor Douven, Michael Dummett, Leon Horsten, Per Martin-Löf, Charles Parsons, Stig Andur Pedersen, Ron Rood, Göran Sundholm, Richard Tieszen, Robert Tragesser, Anne Troelstra, Wim Veldman, and Palle Yourgrau. Finally, I thank series editor Daniel Kolak for his support and patience. Nothing in the following pages should be held against these people.

Leuven   MvA
2002

Chapter 1

The two acts of intuitionism

> Strictly speaking the construction of intuitive mathematics in itself is an action and not a science.
> Brouwer, 1907

> But what I bring you now is exclusively concerned with the way mathematics is rooted in life, and what therefore the starting points of any theory should be.
> Brouwer to his thesis adviser Korteweg, 1906

Construct the number 2 in your mind. Keep it in memory, and construct the number 3. Add them, and keep the result in memory. Now, construct the number 5. Compare it with the result of the sum you made. You will see that they are the same, so you can judge that $2 + 3 = 5$, and write the result in your notebook.

According to Brouwer, all mathematics is like that. 'Intuitionistic mathematics is a mental construction', he wrote [28]. He held that mathematics stands in need of a philosophical foundation, and that intuitionistic mathematics, which he sometimes conveniently called 'modern mathematics', is the only philosophically sound way to do mathematics. In this chapter, we will have a closer look at what constitutes the very essence of intuitionistic mathematics. As this essence determines how mathematics is related to language, truth, and logic, something will be said about these relations as well. The remaining chapters will then address, at a less general level, some unique philosophical aspects of intuitionism and their mathematical consequences.

Here is a second example of the intuitionistic way of looking at mathematics. Unlike the first, it is a negative example, showing something that, intuitionistically, does not work. We will consider the following problem, not for the intrinsic interest it may have, but because it easily lends itself to illustrating a characteristic trait of intuitionistic thought and its formulation is quickly grasped: are there irrational numbers a and b such that a^b is a rational number? In classical mathematics, one may reason as follows. Either $\sqrt{2}^{\sqrt{2}}$ is rational, or it is not. If it is rational, then we can answer the question in the affirmative by setting $a = b = \sqrt{2}$. If it is not rational, let $a = \sqrt{2}^{\sqrt{2}}$ and $b = \sqrt{2}$; then $a^b = (\sqrt{2}^{\sqrt{2}})^{\sqrt{2}} = \sqrt{2}^2 = 2$, which is rational. Either way, we have a solution. But which of the two obtains? The reasoning does not show what the value of a should be. It does not give us a construction for a. Intuitionistically, this argument is therefore not acceptable. For an intuitionist, to say that two numbers a and b as required exist, is to say that we have a mental construction for them; for there is no mathematics outside what we construct in the mind.[1]

One will have guessed from this example that intuitionistic logic must be different from classical logic. In the classical reasoning we used the principle of the excluded middle: a number is either rational, or it is not. But this did not lead to a construction of a specific a and b, which, on the other hand, is the only thing an intuitionist has use for here. A statement will be true when we have an appropriate construction; it will be false when we can show that such a construction is impossible. But otherwise there is nothing to be said about truth or falsity of a statement. Intuitionistic logic therefore never allows one to make claims that one cannot make good on by exhibiting a mathematical construction that shows the object(s) involved in the claim the way they are claimed to be.

In particular, a claim $\exists x P(x)$ to the effect that there exists an object that has property p can only be justified by indicating a construction for such an object, that is, instructions how to build one. And the same principle governs negation: $\neg \exists x P(x)$ must mean that it is contradictory to assume that an a can be constructed such that $P(a)$ holds. Nothing less will do; as mathematical objects do not enjoy an independent existence, nothing outside our constructions will determine whether they have or lack a given property. This means that an object is given by specifying a construction for it, and only so, and therefore the primary notion of identity in intuitionism is that of intensional identity: if two objects are given by the same construction they are intensionally identical, otherwise different, even though in some relevant ways they may still be the same.

The intuitionistic view of logic makes it dependent on mathematics, and not, as the classical conception has it, the other way around. Brouwer came to reject certain principles from classical logic because he construed mathematics differently; it is not the case that he came to construe mathematics differently because he rejected certain principles from classical logic. The intuitionistic endeavour therefore will be entirely misunderstood if construed as primarily concerned with the cogency of certain proof methods or principles of logic; the first concern is rather with mathematical constructions.

The constructions that Brouwer has in mind are based on the intuition of time, as in Kant. Mathematics deals with purely formal objects; like Kant, Brouwer held that time is required for thinking of any object whatsoever. It then becomes plausible to base mathematics on time. Unlike Kant, Brouwer made a sharp distinction between subjective time (inner time consciousness) and objective or scientific time (time as it figures in physics and that you can see on a clock). Mathematics according to Brouwer is based on subjective time. We will have occasion further to discuss Brouwer and Kant in the chapter 6, on intersubjectivity; what should be said now is that, in spite of certain differences between their conceptions of the intuition of time, the function of this intuition with respect to mathematics is the same for Kant and Brouwer. It is the fundamental given out of which all the rest is developed.

Brouwer did not borrow from Kant the pure intuition of space, for he held that the discovery of non-Euclidian geometry had shown that the notion of such an intuition is meaningless. Geometry is instead taken care of by the device of coordinates. Nevertheless, we do have a direct intuition of a continuum, but this is the continuum formed by the flow of time. Our prime intuition of a continuum according to Brouwer is not spatial but temporal.

The intuition of time is part of prelinguistic consciousness. Mathematics, therefore, is essentially languageless. It studies non-linguistic constructions out of something that is not of a linguistic nature.

From the characterization given so far, one can already see the main differences between intuitionism and formalism, and between intuitionism and platonism. Unlike formalism, intuitionism does not hold that mathematics is primarily a matter of language. Unlike platonism, intuitionism does not hold that mathematics is concerned with a realm of objects that exists independently of us; instead, it is about constructions in the mind. In this sense, intuitionistic mathematics is free: it is not constrained by anything outside the mind. The subject creates the mathematical universe and is alone responsible for it. (Had Sartre ever taken the trouble to look into the philosophy of mathematics, he might have liked intuitionism.)

Correspondingly, the intuitionist positions the locus of certainty differently. For a formalist, it is on paper; for a platonist, in an independent realm of abstract objects; for an intuitionist, certainty is only to be found in the mind. The certainty of our mathematical thought is not accounted for in terms of something outside of it, be it a language or a realm of objects, but in terms of the mind's own structure. (That this does not mean that intuitionism is a chapter of psychology is defended in chapter 6.)

A further difference is that the platonist and the formalist try to give a philosophical account of classical mathematics. In principle, the intuitionist is indifferent whether mathematics as founded on his notion of construction happens to coincide with classical mathematics or not; what counts for the intuitionist is the solidity of the philosophical basis. However, the negative example above, the one involving $\sqrt{2}^{\sqrt{2}}$, already indicates that it is not obvious that intuitionism can accept all of classical mathematics; and in fact, intuitionism turns out to limit classical mathematics in some respects, while extending it in others. The limiting aspect was obvious right from the beginning in 1907, when Brouwer defended his doctoral dissertation 'On the foundations of mathematics' at the University of Amsterdam. The second aspect became clear only around 1916–1917, when Brouwer introduced a new kind of object into mathematics, the choice sequence, and developed a form of constructive analysis from it which is at least as rich as classical analysis. Given that choice sequences are not acceptable entities in classical mathematics, it should not be surprising that it is in the theory of real numbers that one finds results that are intuitionistically true but classically false. Intuitionistic mathematics, then, is a thoroughly revisionistic enterprise. In the following chapters we will see various examples of classical principles that cannot be upheld in intuitionism, and of intuitionistic principles that have no place in classical mathematics. The intuitionist is willing to go to such lenghts in the interest of obtaining a form of mathematics that has a solid philosophical foundation.

To arrive at the intuitionistic conception of mathematics one has to perform what Brouwer called 'the two acts of intuitionism' [32, pp.140–141 and 142]:

> The first act of intuitionism separates mathematics from mathematical language, in particular from the phenomena of language which are described by theoretical logic, and recognizes that intuitionist mathematics is an essentially languageless activity of the mind having its origin in the perception of a move of time, i.e. the falling apart of a life moment into two distinct things, one of which gives way to the other, but is retained by memory. If the two-ity thus born is divested of all quality, there remains the empty form of the common substratum of all two-ities. It is this common substratum, this empty form, which is the basic intuition of mathematics.

> The second act of intuitionism ... recognizes the possibility of generating new mathematical entities:
> firstly in the form of infinitely proceeding sequences $p_1, p_2, \ldots$, whose terms are chosen more or less freely from mathematical entities previously acquired ... ;
> secondly in the form of mathematical species, i.e. properties supposable for mathematical entities previously acquired, and satisfying the condition that, if they hold for a certain mathematical entity, they also hold for all mathematical entities which have been defined to be equal to it, relations of equality having to be symmetric, reflexive, and transitive; mathematical entities previously acquired for which the property holds are called elements of the species.

All of intuitionistic mathematics so far has been developed from just these two acts. There is no principled reason why no further acts can be introduced, the sole criterion being that a fundamental insight into the basic intuition has been arrived at. This is one sense in which intuitionistic mathematics is open-ended. I mentioned that part of the second act, the choice sequences, was added a decade after the first act had in effect been performed by Brouwer. It took him some time to discern that the intuition of two-ity also allows for choice sequences. In 1947 [28] and in an appendix to the Cambridge Lectures [37, p.93], Brouwer makes it clear that the possibility of choice sequences is just a consequence of the first act. In other words, the first act gives us a notion of sequence that is more general than that of an algorithmic or lawlike one.

Brouwer says that basic notions such as 'continuous', 'entity', 'once more', 'and so on', are 'immediately conceived in the basic intuition or intuition of the continuum' and therefore irreducible [11, p.179]. In a handwritten note in his own copy of his thesis, Brouwer explained that these notions are just so many different 'polarizations' of the basic intuition [45, p.136]. Thus, each basic notion arises from isolating a certain aspect of the basic intuition that comes to the fore when taking a different perspective on it. When Brouwer introduced choice sequences, he was just polarizing the basic intuition in a way that he hadn't seen was possible before.

Brouwer came to call the actor in the two acts 'the creating subject'.[2] On Brouwer's view, mathematical practice is answerable to the creating subject, not the other way around; and intuitionistic mathematics therefore can be considered nothing but an elaboration of the notion of the creating subject. The nature of this subject I will try further to determine in chapter 6. This task is postponed till the last chapter so that we can first see, in chapters 2 to 5, what the creating subject is supposed to accomplish. In the remainder of the present chapter, I wish to make some general comments on the two acts.

1.1 Ontology

What mathematical objects do the two acts provide the subject with?

The natural numbers Out of the intuition of time—the experience that time is flowing on—the numbers 1 and 2 are created, simultaneously. What Brouwer calls the 'two-ity' is the pure form of the experience 'then–now'. The 'then' corresponds to 1, the 'now' to 2. But the 'now' or present doesn't last. It sinks back into the past to give way to a new present. Thus, as time passes on, the second element of a two-ity itself falls apart into two, embedding a new two-ity in the old one. This way we arrive at 3, and, continuing that way, at the other natural numbers. Brouwer points out that it is necessary to have a two-ity as starting point, and not a unity:

> The first act of construction has *two* discrete things thought together (also according to Cantor ...); F. Meyer ... says that *one* thing is sufficient, because the circumstance that I think of it can be added as a second thing; this is false, for exactly this *adding* (i.e. setting it while the former is retained) *presupposes the intuition of two-ity*; only afterwards this simplest mathematical system is projected on the first thing and the *ego which thinks the thing.* [11, p.179]; original emphasis]

The ability to think two discrete things together—unifying them yet keeping them separate—is the basis of all exact thinking, and this ability is founded on the intuition of time.

denumerable ordinals The very insight that this process of embedding two-ities can be iterated gives rise to the infinite ordinal ω (the first number after 1,2,3,...). This infinity has to be thought of as potential and not actual: on the one hand, the creating subject can start a potentially infinite task, but on the other hand, it can not complete it. From ω one gets further countable ordinals, for example $\omega + 1$ by taking ω and 1 together in a two-ity. A rigorous development of the ordinals requires Brouwer's version of well-ordering; we will have a brief look at that in chapter 4.

The continuum In his late formulations of the two acts, such as the one quoted above from 1952, Brouwer is not as explicit as he was in his thesis from 1907 about the fact that the basic intuition not only yields discreteness but also continuity. This is what is 'between' the elements of a two-ity; it is the abstract form of the time that flows between 'then' and 'now'. Brouwer insisted that discreteness and continuity are mutually dependent and irreducible notions. The creating subject has a direct intuition of the continuum. The circumstance that it is given makes it possible to accept, intuitionistically, this one actual infinity [11, p.176]. But it cannot be constructed out of elements; to model the continuum and be able to analyse it, Brouwer therefore had to introduce choice sequences.

Choice sequences A choice sequence is a potentially infinite sequence of mathematical objects, chosen, one after the other, by the creating subject. Such a sequence is never finished and may be subjected to various conditions. We will have a closer look at choice sequences and their use in analysing the continuum in chapter 3, and at related topics in chapters 4 and 5.

Species Species are an intuitionistic analogue to Cantorian sets. In a species, entities that share a certain property are collected. Like the other objects on this list, species are, in Brouwer's words, a 'modality of the self-unfolding of the primordial intuition of mathematics' [126, p.337]. This follows from Brouwer's conception what a property is:

> Often it is quite simple to construct inside such a structure [or mathematical system], independently of how it originated, new structures, as the elements of which we take elements of the original structure or systems of these, arranged in a new way, but bearing in mind their original arrangement. The so-called 'properties' of a system express the possibility of constructing such new systems having a certain connection with the given system. [11, pp.77–78]

The two systems in question have to be thought together in order to establish a certain connection between them. But holding two separate things together is precisely what the primordial intuition, that of two-ity, is about. Previously constructed entities that have been shown to share a certain property are the elements of a species. Species can also have other species as elements, giving rise to species of higher order. An important difference with Cantorian sets is that species are intensional objects and cannot be identified with their elements: differently defined Cantorian sets may have exactly the same elements and are in that case considered identical (axiom of extensionality), on the other hand the identity of a species consists in the way it is defined.

1.2 Possible cardinalities

'It is introspectively realized,' as Brouwer would put it, that from the two acts one obtains finite species, denumerably infinite species, and the continuum. Are there others?

Brouwer accepted Cantor's diagonal method to show that the real numbers are not denumerable, and also devised an alternative proof using choice sequences (see chapter 3). But he did not conclude from the non-denumerability as much as Cantor did, namely, the existence of a higher number class. Brouwer could not follow in this. Iterating the embedding of two-ities cannot reach beyond the finite and the denumerable, so it is impossible to construct larger entities. As for Brouwer existence can only be analysed in terms of constructions, he naturally concludes that larger entities do not exist. Where Cantor goes on to introduce, beyond $\aleph_0$—indicating the size of the set of natural numbers— the cardinals $\aleph_1, \aleph_2, \ldots$ —indicating the size of bigger sets—Brouwer comments, 'Here Cantor loses contact with the firm ground of mathematics' [11, p.146]. In his view, Cantor had just invented a language to which no mathematical reality corresponds, because the objects figuring in it cannot be constructed from the two acts of intuitionism. There is, moreover, no guarantee whatsoever that a language severed from mathematical intuition is consistent, and Brouwer held language responsible for the paradoxes [11, p.152]. But intuitionism was not developed in reaction to the paradoxes; and even if there had not been any, Brouwer philosphical motivation wouldn't have lost any of its force.

However, Brouwer accepted as a manner of speaking the additional cardinality 'denumerably unfinished':

> We call a set [i.e., species] denumerably unfinished if it has the following properties: we can never construct in a well-defined way more than a denumerable subset of it, but when we have constructed such a subset, we can immediately deduce from it, following some previously defined mathematical process, new elements which are counted to the original set. But from a strictly mathematical point of view this set does not exist as a whole, nor does its power exist; however we can introduce these words here as an expression for a known intention. [11, p.148]

For example, the totality of the definable points on the continuum is denumerably unfinished—this is just what Cantor's diagonal proof shows: there is a procedure that adds, to every denumerable set supposed to contain all real numbers, a real number that had been left out. Brouwer doesn't seem to have had much use for the concept, except in criticizing earlier constructivists, who accepted only definable real numbers: 'such an ever-unfinished and ever-denumerable system of "real numbers" is incapable of fulfilling the mathematical functions of the continuum, for the simple reason that it cannot have a measure positively differing from zero' [32, p.140]. Brouwer considered what he called a denumerably unfinished species really a method (to generate successively denumerably infinite species) rather than a genuine species [13].

With the introduction of spreads, a special kind of species of choice sequences, intuitionism became able to treat certain non-denumerable systems as well, such as the species of all (i.e., both definable and not definable) real numbers, or the (intuitionistic) powerset of $\mathbb{N}$. It is, however, not possible to construct these species as a completed entity in any sense. (Spreads will be treated in chapter 4.)

1.3 Intuition

The development of intuitionistic mathematics consists in making constructions starting from the basic intuition:

> The only possible foundation of mathematics must be sought in this construction under the obligation carefully to watch which constructions intuition allows and which not. [11, p.77]

What intuition allows need not be immediately clear. It takes an exploration. Knowing the ultimate ground of mathematical truths—knowing the basic intuition—does not mean that one thereby knows all that can be obtained from it. One has to see what principles are valid and which are not. This takes thought and, in some sense, experimenting. In this respect, intuitionism is no different from platonism. It is therefore easy to see that Brouwer would have agreed with Gödel who said:

> To apply a position beyond its limit of validity is the most vicious way of discrediting it. This is also true of the emphasis on intuition: appealing to intuition calls for more caution and more experience than the use of proofs—not less. [140, p.301]

Note that Brouwer's intricate analyses such as his proof of the bar theorem (ch.4) would never have been possible, nor needed, if his notion of intuition was anything like the everyday one; nor is it in any way mystical.

I mention this, because sometimes difficulties in understanding intuitionistic mathematics are related to the lifelong, lively interest in both theory and practice of mysticism that Brouwer indeed had. Not many papers by professional mathematicians will contain both mathematical proofs and several passages from the Bhagavad-Gita, as Brouwer's 'Consciousness, Philosophy and mathematics' [29] does. Yet it is not unimportant to be aware that his actual mathematics never makes any use of whatever mystical insights he may have had. What is more, such insights can be of no use in mathematics. That is not my judgement, it is Brouwer's. According to Brouwer, the intuition of time, on which mathematics is based, is a free-will phenomenon that can be discarded at will, and should be, if any mystical insight is to be had. I mentioned that he held that the intuition of time is necessary to be able to think about any object at all; this intuition introduces the subject-object distinction (see chapter 6), and thereby keeps consciousness away from its 'deepest home' [12, 29, 4]. So on Brouwer's view, mathematics is in a sense the very opposite of mysticism. This also means that to accept the intuitionistic view of mathematics, one only needs to share Brouwer's positive ideas about time. His mysticism has no role to play here.

In the exploration of the basic intuition, certain idealizations are made. Intuitionism is a theory not about any thinking subject but about a correctly thinking one [99, p.159]. This means that the object of study is what is intrinsic to the self-unfolding of the basic intuition, and therefore only essential and no accidental features of the subject are studied. Limitations of time, memory, attention and so on are abstracted from. The subject studied is an 'ideal subject', ideal in a way not unlike an 'ideal surface' or 'ideal fluid' in physics.

A platonist may in fact agree that mathematics is a mental activity. And the platonist and the intuitionist will also agree that this activity is not arbitrary. As Gödel observed,

> Brouwer does not mean arbitrary creations. Rather he means creation according to certain principles. The central and appropriate concept for Brouwer is construction rather than creation. We construct something out of something given ... Creation in this sense does not exclude Platonism. [139, p.248]

But this is platonism in a weaker sense than usual; for whereas for the intuitionist the nature of the mental activity is wholly determined by the mind, for the traditional platonist it is determined by the mind and an independent reality which the mind tries to grasp. The classical problem for the platonist is to explain how one has epistemic access to that independent reality. In contrast, intuitionistic mathematics is all in the mind; and this seems to give it an advantage in explaining what the objects of mathematics are and how one can come to know them.

1.4 Truth

Correspondingly, compared to the platonist's, the intuitionist's notion of truth is rather thin:

> Truth is only in reality i.e., in the present and past experiences of consciousness ... But expected experiences, and experiences attributed to others are true only as anticipations and hypotheses; in their contents there is no truth ... There are no non-experienced truths. [29, p.1243]

To experience a truth is to experience that a certain construction has succeeded. This experience may be either direct, in case the subject has actually carried out the construction, or indirect, in case the subject sees that a certain construction method will, if followed through, give the direct experience sought after. Such indirect experiences, which are not merely 'expected' if that is meant to exclude 'guaranteed', are the domain of proofs and logic, which will be the subject of chapter 2.

For Brouwer, that a truth is 'intuitive' or 'given in experience' does not mean that it is 'self-evident' in a Cartesian sense, as is suggested by Körner [98, p.136]. As van Stigt replies to this suggestion,

> Self-evidence implies complete elimination of effort on the part of the subject, the evidence being supplied by and intrinsic to the known object. Apart from the fact that Brouwer never uses the word 'self-evident', he did not recognize 'truths-in-themselves' (e.g. [29, p.1243] and [35, p.113]). [126, p.157]

Brouwer acknowledged that much of intuitionistic mathematics is not at all self-evident in this sense:

> In general intuitionism brings about a complete recasting of mathematics, with the result, to our regret, that in many places its supple and elegant character is lost, and it has to assume much harsher, more tortuous and more complicated forms. Alas, the spheres of truth are less transparent than those of illusion. [26, p.444]

And, when in 1952 he corrected earlier results of his own from 1919, he wrote,

> Reading over these developments to-day, one finds that they are obsolete and in need of radical recasting. We must acquiesce to the fact that intuitionistic ideas penetrate mathematics slowly and that remnants of unclear classical ways of thinking are only gradually removed. [33, p.516]

What 'intuitive' or 'given' means for Brouwer is that there are no intermediaries, in particular not in the form of language (logic); but it is not meant to suggest indubitability. I am suggesting, then, that Brouwer's epistemology is best construed as what is nowadays known as a fallibilist foundationalism.

Finally, that truth can be found only in the subject's experience of its own constructional activities by no means implies that the subject can never be surprised at what it finds. In his 1907 thesis, Brouwer speaks of 'the exploration of a structure built by [one]self', which he contrasts with the chain of logical deductions that may be a linguistic accompaniment to it [11, p.135]. This exploration proceeds 'from clearly perceived relations (i.e. substructures) to new relations which were not immediately perceived'.[3] There is nothing odd about the possibility that by analysis of its own constructions the subject comes to see properties of them that it may not have noticed before.

1.5 The role of language

'Formal language accompanies mathematics as the weather-map accompanies the atmospheric processes,' Brouwer said [40, p.451].[4] Language must remain secondary, as mathematical constructions themselves are effected without words:

> Strictly speaking the construction of intuitive mathematics in itself is an *action* and not a *science*; it only becomes a science ... in a mathematics of the second order, which consists of the *mathematical consideration of mathematics* or *of the language of mathematics* [11, p.99, original emphasis]

And however exact a language may be, if our thinking is not, under appropriate conditions, capable of matching that exactness, the language is of no use in doing mathematics. For we would then have no reason to assume that the language does what it is supposed to do. A specific example is that without an intuitive grasp of induction, one wouldn't be able to work with formal systems. But induction is just one polarization of the unfolding of the two-ity. In that sense, Brouwer argued, a language for mathematics 'needs the basic intuition of mathematics as much as mathematics itself needs it' [11, p.180]. Formal systems presuppose certain intuitions and cannot replace intuiton altogether.[5] In practice, language does much to lift the burden of mathematical thinking; but it cannot serve as a foundation for it. The exactness and correctness of mathematics is to be found in the primordial intuition and its unfolding [26, p.443].

Intuitionists therefore disagree with formalists, who hold that mathematics is a matter of language, even (partly, or, in the first version of Hilbert's program, wholly) meaningless language. As Brouwer bluntly put it:

> It is equally stupid and simple to consider mathematics to be just an axiom system as it is to see a tree as nothing but a quantity of planks. [126, p.284]

Brouwer is suggesting here a contrast between language, which is as dead as planks, and mathematics, which is alive like a tree; we will see him use the metaphor of being alive again in this connection in the next section.

In 1927, Brouwer presented a refined, proof-theoretic version of his argument that mathematics is not essentially linguistic [67, p.460, footnote 8]. Language, whether interpreted or uninterpreted, yields finite linguistic objects. But for reasons we will see in chapter 2, Brouwer held that mental proofs are often infinite. It then follows that mental proofs cannot be linguistic in nature. At that time, Brouwer said that this was his main argument against Hilbert's formalism.

In many ways, the intuitionistic and platonistic views on mathematics are opposites. The former locates the reality of mathematics in languageless constructions in the mind, the latter in a realm of abstract objects outside the mind. However, in doing so, they both stress that mathematics is not, at root, of a linguistic nature. Language can only have a descriptive function and not a creative one. It is not surprising, then, to find that Gödel's general view on language and mathematics is very similar to Brouwer's:

> We do not have any primitive intuition about language ... Everything has to be proved [when we are dealing with language]. The overestimation of language is deplorable. [140, p.180]

> Language is useful and even necessary for fixing our ideas. But this is a purely practical affair. [140, p.180]

The practical role of language in intuitionism is to help to record and remember mathematical activity, for one's own benefit, and for communicating it to other people. The two functions of memorizing and communicating resemble one another, as Gilbert Ryle saw: a thinker is a teacher who is his own student [122].[6] But someone with a perfect memory could do exact mathematics in solitude without any need for language.

Brouwer thought that language is always to some extent inexact, and that 'in spite of its efficiency it can never completely safeguard us against misunderstanding' [28]. But precisely because of his perception of the limitations of language, in mathematics and elsewhere, Brouwer was well aware of the need to be as exact as possible in one's use of it, so as to minimize the unavoidable misunderstandings. Such were his reasons to help founding the 'Signific Movement' in Holland, a movement for language reform inspired by the 'significs' of the English Lady Welby. Among its aims were:

> 1. To coin words of spiritual value for the languages of western nations and thus make those spiritual values enter into their mutual understanding;

> 2. To point out and brand those words of the principal languages which falsely suggest spiritual tendencies for ideas ultimately originating in the desire for material safety and comfort, and in so doing to purify and to correct the aims of democracy towards a universal commonwealth with exclusive administrative function. [27, p.201]

These are of particular interest to understanding intuitionistic mathematics, for, as van Stigt has pointed out,

> They are the two aspects of Brouwer's Signific programme, the two aspects also of his Intuitionist programme, a diagnostic one and a creative one: first, to diagnose the misuse of language and the tyranny of language in distorting the underlying deeper reality, causing the birth of deformed ideas and repressing the birth of pure ones; secondly, a creative one, in generating a new language, new words, truthfully reflecting the pure human thought and though processes. [125, p.509]

In that sense, principled intuitionism, for all its misgivings about language, may even be conceived of as a study of language. Intuitionism then is a critique of the role of language in mathematics and of words such as 'number', 'point', 'continuum', 'not', in particular.[7]

1.6 The place of logic

Chapter 2 will be concerned with the particular principles of intuitionistic logic; the present section with Brouwer's view of the place of logic as such.

Brouwer considered logic to be a special language. It merely describes the regularities we find in reports of mathematical activities; in other words, it is an application of mathematics to mathematical discourse. Logic is therefore in a certain sense an empirical affair. Brouwer reckoned with the possibility that different cultures have different logics, even as their mathematics is the same, because the human intellect is organized the same way (this sameness is a theme that we will return to in chapter 6).[8] Logic belongs to etnography [11, p.130]. To a certain extent this applies to today's discussions whether the true language of mathematics is that of first-order logic, second order logic, or Hintikka's IF logic. But according to Brouwer, *the* true language does not exist, for all logical notions we derive a posteriori by observing our own mathematical activity, which is open-ended.

Because, as we saw in the previous section, language can have no foundational role in intuitionistic mathematics, in particular logic cannot. It is not that Brouwer has something against logic as such; he is not, as I once heard a famous philosopher describe him, 'an anti-logician'. But Brouwer warns against misunderstanding what logic can accomplish. It has a descriptive function, but not a creative one. Formal logic as such has little to do with advancing one's understanding of mathematics. This is why Brouwer *did* call himself, in a draft from the late 20s, an 'alogicist' [43, p.303]. He disagreed with the logicists, such as Frege and Russell, who tried to found mathematics on logic. From Brouwer's point of view, that is putting the cart before the horse. Logic describes regularities in mathematical activity, but it does not bring about such activity:

> Logic is not a reliable instrument to discover truths and cannot deduce truths which would not be accessible in another way as well ... Mathematics rigorously treated from this point of view, and deducing theorems exclusively by means of introspective construction, is called intuitionistic mathematics. [29, p.1243]

But once a certain logical principle is intuitionistically justified, it is possible to use that principle mindlessly while having the guarantee that to the end result corresponds a mathematical construction [12, 32]. The thing to keep in mind is that the direction of justification always is from mathematics to logic.

Just as logic results from a mathematical study of reports on mathematical constructional activities, logic in turn can be studied mathematically. In his thesis, Brouwer describes in detail an infinite hierarchy of mathematical activities, their linguistic accompaniments, and the mathematical study of those linguistic structures [11, pp.173–175]. This leads to mathematics of first, second, etc.

order; in effect, Brouwer here introduced in a very precise manner the distinction, better known from later work by Hilbert, Bernays and Tarski, between mathematics and metamathematics, between language and metalanguage. It was Brouwer who, during a meeting with Hilbert that took place in the Dutch seaside resort of Scheveningen in 1909 and which Brouwer later described as 'a beautiful new ray of light through my life', introduced these ideas to Hilbert [42, pp.128–129]. Their importance was not lost on Hilbert, who made good use of them in the mature version of his formalistic program.[9]

But to metamathematical results, such as proofs of consistency, completeness, or incompleteness, the intuitionist attaches a different and less dramatic importance than others do. Such proofs are all about linguistic systems; they have no direct mathematical meaning. For example, about consistency proofs Brouwer said:

> The consistency of the axioms does not involve the existence of the corresponding mathematical system. Even if the mathematical system of reasonings exists, this does not entail that it is *alive*, i.e. that it accompanies a sequence of thoughts, and even if the latter is the case, this sequence of thoughts need not be a *mathematical* development, so it need not be convincing. [11, p.138, original emphasis]

> An incorrect theory, even if it cannot be inhibited by any contradiction that would refute it, is none the less incorrect, just as a criminal policy is none the less criminal even if it cannot be inhibited by any court that would curb it.[10] [17, p.336]

In turn, Gödel's completeness theorem for first-order logic can be said to construct a model only in a much weaker sense of that term than the intuitionist asks for. The 'construction' makes essential use of classical logic. The Dutch intuitionist Veldman [136] has given an intuitionistically acceptable completeness proof for intuitionistic first-order logic without $\bot$ ('falsum', a proposition that is always false); to extend that result to full logic requires an interpretation of $\bot$ that does not square with its intended intuitionistic meaning, as Veldman readily conceded (see also the discussion in [49, section 5.7]).

Gödel's incompleteness theorems did not surprise Brouwer (who will have appreciated their beauty, see the quote at the end of chapter 2). According to Freudenthal, Brouwer commented that, on contentual grounds, he had always expected the insufficiency of formal systems [45, p.359]. Given the context of incompleteness, what Brouwer refers to here probably is his conviction that mathematical constructional activity is always open-ended. There may be an interesting analogy between Brouwer's reaction to Gödel's theorem and Gödel's reaction to Turing's argument that mental procedures cannot go beyond mechanical procedures. Both Brouwer and Gödel point out that, in Gödel's words, 'mind, in its use, is not static, but constantly developing, i.e., that we understand abstract terms more and more precisely as we go on using them, and that more and more abstract terms enter the sphere of our understanding' [60, p.306].

In several respects, though certainly not all, the philosophical ethos of Brouwer and Gödel was the same: proudly at odds with the spirit of their times, highly independent, stressing intuition, sceptical of the powers of language, and rejecting naturalistic, materialistic, and mechanistic philosophies. Yet personally they do not seem to have particularly liked each other. Brouwer had dinner at the Gödel's on his visit to the Institute for Advanced Study in Princeton in 1953; Gödel's report in a letter to his mother does not give the impression that the host had much enjoyed the evening [45, p.475]. The logician Georg Kreisel, for a long time a close friend of Gödel's, confirms that 'Gödel was utterly bored by Brouwer unlike several logicians and mathematicians who, being dry themselves, were buoyed by Brouwer's probably genuine exuberance' [100, p.146]; Brouwer in turn sent, in a letter from 1955 to Morse, his best wishes to several named people at the Institute, but did not mention Gödel.[11]

The considerations in this chapter are the starting point of Brouwer's explanations what mathematical statements mean and what makes some of them true. Even simple cases such as $2+3 = 5$ require going to considerable philosophical depths, but it is certainly worth the effort to do so. For, as Brouwer wrote, 'Research in foundations of mathematics is inner inquiry with revealing and liberating consequences'. 'Also,' he added enigmatically, 'in non-mathematical domains of thought.' [29, p.1249]

Chapter 2

Proofs and logic

Mathematics is first of all an activity of constructing starting from the two acts described in the previous chapter. For Brouwer, as we saw, to say that a proposition p is true means that the truth of p has been experienced. A proof, then, primarily is a sequence of mental acts in which a certain experience was brought about. Brouwer's student Heyting put it thus:

> If mathematics consists of mental constructions, then every mathematical theorem is the expression of a result of a succesful construction. The proof of the theorem consists in this construction itself, and the steps of the proof are the same as the steps of the mathematical construction. [74, p.107]

As mathematics is essentially languageless, the same can be said about proofs. In its most fundamental sense, the notion of proof has nothing to do with either formal systems or logic.

In acts of reflection, the subject can look back on its activities and single out a certain episode. Thus thematized, the episode once lived is considered as an object (an objectified proof; the inviting 'proof object' nowadays is used in a more specific meaning). The subject can study and come back to this object time and again.[12] In chapter 4, we will see how Brouwer capitalized on the notion of proofs as objects in order to show a purely mathematical result; and, as we will see below, intuitionistic logic depends entirely on that notion.

A proof object lends itself to description in a language, yielding a linguistic proof. A linguistic proof accompanies a constructional activity but cannot definitively replace it. A linguistic proof can also serve as an instruction (to oneself, for future reference, or to others) that is guaranteed to bring about that experience.

Of course not just any selection of the subject's activities assembles into a proof. A proof is a selection that strongly coheres in virtue of the various parts being dependent on each other according to the construction principles recognized by the subject. So when the sequence of acts in question is objectified, one obtains an object with a clear internal structure. Brouwer thematized that structure and found that it is always inductively generated ('well-ordered', on his understanding of that term, to be explained in chapter 4) and often infinite. Let us see why this should be so.

In a proof, one shows that certain relations hold between certain mathematical objects. These relations can be decomposed into basic relations; correspondingly, the inferences in any proof can be decomposed into elementary inferences, starting from elementary facts (0-step inferences, that is, axioms in the original sense of the word). A complete decomposition of an ordinary proof into elementary inferences results in a mental proof that Brouwer calls its canonical form.

That a mental proof in general contains infinitely many terms is seen as follows. Most ordinary proofs at some point contain a universally quantified proposition $\forall x P(x)$, a proof of which is specified by a method that, given any a, provides us with a proof of $P(a)$. In passing, note that, accordingly, the strict notion of proof may be extended to include methods to generate strict proofs. To understand the method in question is to understand that for any a we can, when asked, prove $P(a)$. Thus, the method is directed toward the infinitely many proofs $P(0), P(1), P(2), \ldots$. A canonical proof contains all these proofs instead of their summary statement $\forall x P(x)$, and whatever in the ordinary proof is inferred from that summary is in the canonical proof inferred from these infinitely many premises.

It would not be correct to think of a canonical proof as one in which every proof implicitly referred to in the ordinary proof is actually carried out. For in that case, the canonical proof would be an actually infinite structure; but such a structure cannot be constructed out of elements on the basis of the two acts of intuitionism. Truth of a proposition will not be experienced as a result of actually carrying out all the parts of a canonical proof, and a canonical proof therefore is not a proof in the primary sense as defined at the beginning of this chapter. Rather, a canonical proof reflects the inner structure of the complex thought that is the ordinary proof. The sense in which a canonical proof contains infinitely many elements is that of implicit reference, or, in Husserl's term, intentional implication. The decomposition of an ordinary proof into a canonical one consists in an analysis of the intentional structure of the former.

The infinity of this structure prohibits a direct expression of it in a language of the sort envisioned in Hilbert's formalism, as expressions in such a language are finite. Mental proofs, Brouwer observes [21, footnote 8], therefore cannot be identified with them. He adds that this remark contains his 'main argument against the claims of Hilbert's metamathematics'. For reasons we saw in chapter 1, he even says that these linguistic expressions 'do not belong to mathematics'. The infinite structure can only be expressed indirectly, in the form of a method to generate it. The availability of such a method is what makes an infinite canonical proof tractable, intuitionistically.

The concept of a canonical proof is essential to Brouwer's proof of the bar theorem, to be discussed in chapter 4; later, different versions of it were adopted by the English philosopher of language Michael Dummett and by the Swedish philosopher and mathematician Martin-Löf.

The fact that the intuitionist is willing to consider proofs as objects that can be referred to in mathematical reasoning, not to mention the infinite structure of proofs, shows that intuitionism is by no means a variety of finitism [8, p.502].

Let us take a closer look at the intuitionistic understanding of how truth and proofs are related. Truth is a temporal notion: a proposition is not true before it has actually been proved. The act of proving it makes it true. This does not mean that before that, the proposition was false; it had no truth value at all.

For example, consider the proposition 'π is irrational'. Lambert proved it in 1761. On Brouwer's view, before 1761, it was not true that π was irrational. How could it have been? On his understanding of truth, that would have meant that the irrationality of π was experienced before 1761; as a matter of historical fact, that is not the case. Of course before 1761 it was not true that π was not irrational: no one had experienced that either.

On the classical conception of truth, there are only two possibilities for a proposition with respect to truth: p is true, or p is false. Intuitionistically, there are four [35, p.114],[37, p.92]:

1. p has been experienced as true

2. p has been experienced as false

3. Neither 1 nor 2 has occurred yet, but we know a procedure to decide p (i.e., a procedure that will prove p or prove $\neg p$)

4. Neither 1 nor 2 has occurred yet, and we do not know a procedure to decide p

It is important to see that cases 3 and 4 are of a different nature than cases 1 and 2. A proposition of case 3 or 4 may, in the course of time, move to case 1 or 2; but once in either case 1 or case 2, it can never change cases anymore. One could well argue, as Brouwer did, that for all purposes, case 3 reduces to 1 or 2. Case 3 is the one where we are allowed to say 'a construction exists' even when we do not yet have carried it out. The inclusion of this indirect case is warranted by Brouwer's statement, in notes to the Cambridge Lectures, 'The case that [p] has neither been proved to be true nor to be absurd, but that we know a finite algorithm leading to the statement either that [p] is true, or that [p] is absurd, obviously is reducible to the first and second cases' [37, p.92]. If this reduction is accepted, then we can say that case 2 corresponds to the strong negation (negation as impossibility of proof) and case 4 to the weak negation (negation as absence of proof).

So in effect there are only three cases to deal with, 1, 2, and 4. But note that the fact that there are three cases, as in classical logic there are two, does not mean that intuitionistic logic, in analogy to classical logic, is thereby a three-valued logic. Weak negation of p only means that we do not have a proof of p now; perhaps we will find one in the future, and then p will be true. Strong negation of p means that it is provably impossible to have a proof of p, come what may (Brouwer's term is 'absurdity' of p). For this reason, strong negation is correlated to the truth value 'false', but weak negation is not correlated to a third truth value. In 1928, Glivenko gave a formal proof of this fact [55], and in 1932, Gödel elegantly demonstrated that not only is intuitionistic logic not a three-valued logic, it is not an n-valued logic for any natural number n [57].[13]

As a consequence of his view that mathematical truth is experienced truth, Brouwer believes that there is an intrinsic time parameter in mathematical truth. Many people believe, unlike Brouwer, that mathematical truths are not tensed but eternal—either because such truths are outside time altogether (atemporal) or because they hold in all time (omnitemporal). Either way, mathematical truths are not temporally differentiated. On such a view, mathematics must also have a different basis than what the subject has experienced.

A classical mathematician, for example, will not make Brouwer's identification of truth and having had the relevant experience, but probably would accept proof, certainly not as what makes a proposition true, but as the only ground for asserting its truth. This identification is not threatened by Gödel's theorem: that theorem is about formalization, hence about (a particular kind of) language. It expresses an inherent limitation to formalization, but not to that which is formalized. (So it is a problem for a radical formalist, who doesn't distinguish between these two.)

The real difference between the classical mathematician and the intuitionist is in their answer to the question: what is a proof? For an intuitionist, a proof consists of steps that preserve constructability; for a classical mathematician, of steps that preserve mind-independent truth. This means that a classical mathematician, to recognize and understand a proof, must make reference to something that the intuitionist can do without. (Heyting turned this into an argument in favour of intuitionism: it doesn't need to make metaphysical hypotheses.)

One can take also take the position that mathematical truth is tenseless, while keeping a constructivist outlook, by saying that the truth of p consists in the tenseless existence of a constructive proof object (as opposed to proof objects that come into being in reflection, as described above), as for example Martin-Löf does. The idea is that we would have the ability to come to know this object, but we may or may not actually do so. A true proposition is true before it has been proved; the act of proving consists in our getting acquainted with a proof object. Brouwer's 'true is what has been experienced (has been proved)' then is replaced by 'true is what could be experienced (is provable)'.

From a Brouwerian point of view three things about the tenseless construal seem problematic .

First, how is this tenseless existence to be explained? Tenseless existence seems to imply the a priori existence of proofs, independent of our activity. For such a realist assertion Brouwer has no place. Perhaps there is an alternative explanation, but it is hard to see how any explanation of tenseless existence can be in harmony with Brouwer's principle 'the only a priori element in science is time' [11, p.99].

Second, what, in any case, is the need for a notion of mathematical truth defined in terms of such independently existing proof objects? In other words, what is the need for a tenseless notion of mathematical truth? It certainly serves to do justice to our intuition that there need not be a connection between the content of a mathematical proposition and the moment at which it is proved; but Brouwer could acknowledge most of that, simply by saying that from inspection of a given proof one sees that it could have been carried out in the same way at an earlier or at a later moment than it actually was. (I am abstracting from choice sequences for the moment.) What he would resist is the idea that it is somehow similarly the case that there are proofs that we have yet to find and about which, once found, we could say that they could just as well have been given now; for on Brouwer's construal of the notion of proof as explained so far, it is impossible for a proof to exist independently of the subject's actual experience.

Third, Brouwer has in fact reason not to use a tenseless notion of truth. This is because he accepts choice sequences as genuine objects. They acquire properties in the course of time, based on free choices made by the subject; a tenseless notion of truth is incompatible with that. For example, if we start a lawless sequence α, there is no fact of the matter what $\alpha(3)$ should be. As soon as we have made a choice n for it, we can prove $\alpha(3) = n$; but it cannot be the case that this was atemporally true, independently of our choice, and that we just came to know some pre-existing proof.

This brings us to the issue of epistemic logic. Clearly, at any moment the possession or lack of certain knowledge is significant to intuitionistic logic as conceived by Brouwer. Yet in so far as epistemic logic is based on a distinction between what is known to be true and what is true, it would be rather misleading to call intuitionistic logic an epistemic logic. For according to Brouwer, truth is always experienced truth, so at no moment there are truths that the subject doesn't know yet. The subject can be ignorant in the sense of not yet having solved an open problem, but not in the sense of not knowing a certain truth. Something similar holds for the objects. As the subject alone is responsible for constructing the objects, the objects are perfectly well known: the subject can indicate at what moment it began to construct them, according to what principles (in chapter 6 I will argue that there is no reason to fear that the subject might be forgetful). A construction need not follow a law; this refers to choice sequences, the possibility of which is guaranteed by the second act of intuitionism. In such a case, that there are open questions is not because of a gap between the truth and our knowledge, but because that object itself is incomplete and always in a state of development (see the example of α in the previous paragraph).

Therefore, the claim that 'Brouwer clearly thought that a mathematical object can be constructive, but not known, viz. when we do not know what the construction law is or when the construction does not follow any law' [79, p.17] is not correct. Of course the subject may form expectations or intentions directed at propositions or objects that it hasn't constructed yet; but that does not suffice to make the intended propositions true or bring the intended objects into existence. One could only say that an object may be constructive yet unknown if one thinks of the object as somehow transcendent to the subject's activity, which, on Brouwer's view, it never is.

In chapter 5, on creating subject arguments, we will have occasion to come back to the differences between tensed and tenseless construals of mathematical truth.

Brouwer always steered clear of a systematic development of logic. Here his student Heyting did the pioneering work, nowadays known as 'the proof interpretation';[14] or rather, that term has come to refer to a close family of interpretations. Heyting described his point of departure as follows:

> We here distinguish between propositions and assertions. An assertion is the affirmation of a proposition. A mathematical proposition expresses a certain expectation. For example, the proposition, 'Euler's constant C is rational', expresses the expectation that we could find two integers a and b such that $C = a/b$. Perhaps the word 'intention', coined by the phenomenologists, expresses even better what is meant here ... The affirmation of a proposition means the fulfillment of an intention. [73, pp.58–59]

Thus, the intention expressed by p is fulfilled exactly if it is known how to prove p by a construction. 'p is true' means 'the intention expressed by p has been fulfilled'. This shows again how Brouwer's conception of truth—phrased here, following Heyting, in Husserl's terms—is different from a tenseless one, where one could say 'p is true exactly if there exists a proof (whether we know it or not)'. To say 'a proof exists (whether we know it or not)' is to make an assertion about something that is allowed to transcend the subject's experience (compare [72, p.307]).

From this general principle of interpretation, the following explanations of the meaning of the logical constants are derived [72, 73].

- conjunction: (the intention expressed by) $p \wedge q$ is fulfilled exactly when p is fulfilled and q is fulfilled.

- disjunction: $p \vee q$ is fulfilled exactly when at least one of p, q is fulfilled.

- implication: $p \rightarrow q$ is fulfilled exactly when the subject has a construction that transforms any construction (proof) of p into one of q.

- negation: $\neg p$ is fulfilled exactly when the subject has a construction that transforms any proof of p into a proof of a contradiction.

- universal quantification: $\forall x A(x)$ is fulfilled exactly when the subject has a construction that assigns to every element d of the domain a proof of $A(d)$.

- existential quantification: $\exists x A(x)$ is fulfilled exactly when the subject has a construction that selects an element d of the domain such that $A(d)$.

One may have noticed that negation is defined as implication of falsum: $\neg p \equiv p \rightarrow \bot$. Thus, intuitionistic negation is not merely a reversal of truth values, but involves the subject's possessing a certain construction method. In that sense, intuitionistic negation is a positive statement. The negation sign '¬' was first introduced by Heyting to distinguish intuitionistic from classical negation, which at the time was often notated as '∼'.

Starting from 1944, G.F.C. Griss, a former student of Brouwer's who was sympathetic to intuitionism, argued that negation should be banished from mathematics (e.g. [65]). His reasoning was as follows. If mathematics is to be based solely on constructions that are given to intuition and in that sense evident, then there is no room for negation. After all, negation is defined as the implication of falsum. As the false can never be evident in the required sense, this means that if the implication $p \to \bot$ holds, construction p is impossible as well. This captures the meaning of negation, but requires the admissibility of hypothetical constructions: 'if we had a construction of p, a contradiction could be derived'. But a hypothetical construction, Griss argued, can never be fully given in intuition (if it were, it would have become an actual construction), certainly not if the hypothesis turns out to be false. But then an understanding of negation asks for an intuition that is impossible.

Brouwer's own reply will be discussed in the chapter on intersubjectivity. It consisted in exhibting a counterexample to Griss' claim, that is, in actually constructing a real number with a property that can only be defined as the negation of some other property. An answer in general terms would be that, to see that one construction is possible on the assumption of another, there is no need actually to carry out the assumed one. It suffices to consider its intentional content or meaning, which can be done in abstraction of any evidence or counterevidence for the construction thus intended. For example, it is by considering the meaning of the term 'square circle' that we see the truth of 'If something is a square circle, then it is a square'. If we did not see this truth, it would be inexplicable how we could come to see that 'square circle' is a contradictory concept. Another example is given below, when discussing the status in intuitionism of the principle 'ex falso sequitur quodlibet'.

In Heyting's explanations of $\to, \neg,$ and $\forall$, a construction is asked for that transforms proofs into other proofs. The creating subject does not need additional verification that such a construction does what it is supposed to do: it will recognize a suitable construction as such, and if it doesn't, then the purported construction doesn't count for that very reason. After all, on Brouwer's view, only the fact that the subject experiences that an object (in this case, the purported construction method) has a certain property makes it true that that object has that property. It is of course not excluded that the subject comes to have experiences that it hadn't expected; perhaps it later on comes to see that a proposed construction will indeed deliver what is required from it.

Heyting had given a formalization of intuitionistically valid principles of logic (not the first, as we will see) in 1927 (in Dutch; published (revised), in German, in 1930 [69, 70, 71]). He had arrived at it by going through the axioms of Whitehead and Russell's Principia Mathematica and crossing out those that were not intuitionistically acceptable.[15] His axioms for propositional logic, for example, are:

$$p \to (p \wedge p) \tag{2.1}$$
$$(p \wedge q) \to (q \wedge p) \tag{2.2}$$
$$(p \to q) \to ((p \wedge r) \to (q \wedge r)) \tag{2.3}$$
$$((p \to q) \wedge (q \to r)) \to (p \to r) \tag{2.4}$$
$$q \to (p \to q) \tag{2.5}$$
$$(p \wedge (p \to q)) \to q \tag{2.6}$$
$$p \to (p \vee q) \tag{2.7}$$
$$(p \vee q) \to (q \vee p) \tag{2.8}$$
$$((p \to r) \wedge (q \to r)) \to ((p \vee q) \to r) \tag{2.9}$$
$$\neg p \to (p \to q) \tag{2.10}$$
$$((p \to q) \wedge (p \to \neg q)) \to \neg p \tag{2.11}$$

Detailed considerations about the exact interpretation, such as we saw above, were given by Heyting only after that. One easily verifies that these 11 axioms all come out true on the proof interpretation, possibly with one exception, which I will come back to later.

Heyting never claimed that his formalization was the definitive intuitionistic logic, and moreover admitted that there could not be one, as 'the possibilities of thought cannot be reduced to a finite number of rules set up in advance' [69, p.311]. But the motto that he had chosen to preface his paper with, 'stones for bread' (Matt. 7:9 and Luke 11:11), has been largely ignored. Heyting's formal system is often incorrectly taken to be the definitive intuitionistic logic. This he deplored:

> I regret that my name is known to-day mainly in connection with these papers, which were very imperfect and contained many mistakes. They were of little help in the struggle to which I devoted my life, namely a better understanding and appreciation of Brouwer's ideas. They diverted the attention from the underlying ideas to the formal system itself. [77, p.15]

This is no less true today than when Heyting wrote it in 1978. Indeed, the reader will find that Heyting's clauses are sometimes given (mathematically fruitful!) interpretations that actually diverge from Brouwer's intentions that Heyting had hoped to clarify.

Although Heyting shared Brouwer's idea that formal language is no more capable of capturing the essence of mathematics than natural language is, he was more optimistic about its value in communication than his teacher. Perhaps Brouwer recognized some of that value, after all: he used his influence to make sure that Heyting's formalization was published in one of the top journals of the time, and gave up on a paper of his own, saying that Heyting's work 'clarifies in a masterly way all the points which I had wanted to clear up' [126, p.291].

There is reason to doubt, however, that Brouwer agreed with all of Heyting's rules; this concerns axiom 10 in the list above, which is the possible exception that I was speaking of. It is a version of 'ex falso sequitur quodlibet': if p is false, then, if it is nevertheless assumed to be true, one can derive everything. Heyting (later) tried to justify the axiom as follows:

> Axiom [10] may not seem intuitively clear. As a matter of fact, it adds to the precision of the definition of implication. You remember that $p \to q$ can be asserted if and only if we possess a construction which, joined to the construction p, would prove q. Now suppose that $\vdash \neg p$, that is, we have deduced a contradiction from the supposition that p were carried out. Then, in a sense, this can be considered as a construction, which, joined to a proof of p (which cannot exist) leads to a proof of q. [75, p.106]

How to assess this attempt at justification?

The problem with axiom 10 is not so much that it asks for a construction (fulfilling q) on the basis of assuming something known to be impossible (if there is a construction fulfilling $\neg p$, then it is impossible to fulfill the intention p).[16] That the difficulty lies elsewhere is clear from the following example: let p be 'The first 10 decimals of π are 0' and q 'The first 9 decimals of π are 0'. Then on the one hand, $\neg p$; on the other, we can certainly indicate a construction that transforms any construction for p into one for q (just ignore the 10th decimal); so $\neg p \to (p \to q)$ for these particular p and q. To repeat what was observed above for negation (a special case of implication): to see that one construction is possible on the assumption of another, it suffices to consider the intentional content or meaning of the latter, which is independent of whether it has been or even could be carried out.

Rather, the problem is the universality that axiom 10 calls for, its claim that anything whatsoever can be proved from a contradiction. To prove is, intuitionistically, to indicate a construction. But it is not clear why the subject should be able to construct, once it has arrived at a contradiction, anything it likes, let alone why there should be a uniform method to do this, as the axiom, in its generality, claims. The apparent looseness of the connection between antecedent and consequent does not go together well with the intuitionistic demand that this connection be established by a construction method. The Russian mathematician Kolmogorov seems to have been right when he said that, just like the principle of excluded middle, the principle of ex falso 'has no intuitive foundation' [67, p.419].[17] Put differently, Kolmogorov in 1925 was asking for what is nowadays known as a 'relevant logic', a logic that respects the demand for a tight connection between premises and conclusion of an argument. That demand accords well with Brouwer's idea that logic in the end only describes regularities in mathematical activity. One therefore has to agree with Hao Wang, who in his introduction to Kolmogorv's paper wrote: 'It is fair to say that, as a codification of Brouwer's ideas, [Kolmogorov's 1925 proposal] is no less reasonable than Heyting's propositional calculus' [67, 414].

In 1932, Kolmogorov saw a way to make axiom 10 acceptable by interpreting propositions as 'problems' and their proofs as 'solutions'. 'As soon as $\neg a$ is solved, then the solution of a is impossible and the problem $a \to b$ is without content' [97, p.331]; 'The proof that a problem is without content [owing to an impossible assumption] will always be considered as its solution' [97, p.329].

Note the contrast with Heyting's attitude, according to which we 'in a sense' do have, given a proof of $\neg a$, a construction that shows $a \to b$, for any b. But while it is meaningful to say that a problem has been solved when it is shown that it cannot be solved (a 'higher-order' solution as familiar from Hilbert's program), for an intention to be fulfilled it will not do to say that a construction exists 'in a sense' while leaving it wholly unspecified. It seems that Kolmogorov's (1932) and Heyting's interpretations are therefore not equivalent (as Heyting later claimed they were [74, p.107]).

In his intuitionistic work, Brouwer never used 'ex falso', and this should not come as a surprise now. The principle seems descriptive of no mathematical activity. Given Brouwer's priority of the activity of mathematics over the linguistic phenomenon of logic, and the role of intentionality in his philosophy of mathematics, perhaps the combination of Kolmogorov's formalization from 1925 with Heyting's interpretation in terms of fulfillment of intentions is, within the limits any linguistic system will have by its very nature, faithful to Brouwer's ideas.

Let us now see some examples of Brouwer's implicit use of the proof interpretation.

In 1923 Brouwer showed that $\neg\neg\neg p \leftrightarrow \neg p$, or rather, that 'absurdity of absurdity of absurdity is equivalent to absurdity'; yet Brouwer's putting it that way is not all pedantry, as what matters to him is the constructions and not their linguistic reports. Here is how Brouwer proved the equivalence (in a later formulation):

> *Firstly*, since implication of the assertion y by the assertion x implies implication of absurdity of x by absurdity of y, the implication of *absurdity of absurdity* by *truth* (which is an established fact) implies the implication of *absurdity of truth*, that is to say of *absurdity, by absurdity of absurdity of absurdity*. *Secondly*, since truth of an assertion implies absurdity of its absurdity, in particular truth of absurdity implies absurdity of absurdity of absurdity. [37, p.12, original emphasis]

Another one of Brouwer's uses of the proof interpretation avant la lettre is his argument from around 1907 that there are no absolutely undecidable propositions, that is, there are no propositions p such that it is impossible to have a proof of either p or $\neg p$. This he shares with Hilbert and Gödel, who in fact believe something stronger, to wit, 'every proposition can be decided'. Constructively, the difference is that between believing that there can be no proposition that is unsolvable by any method whatsoever and believing that there is a method to decide all mathematical propositions (Gödel at some point was convinced that Leibniz had found such a method). Intuitionistically, the latter belief asks for more, in fact, for too much. Brouwer justified his belief as follows:

> Can one ever prove of a proposition, that it can never be decided? No, because one would have to so by reductio ad absurdum. So one would have to say: assume that the proposition has been decided in sense X, and from that deduce a contradiction. But then it would have been proved that not X is true, and the proposition is decided after all. [46, p.174n.a]

Here is how the argument works. On the one hand, the assumption that we have a proof of p leads, by hypothesis, to a contradiction: $p \to \bot$. But according to the clause for negation in the proof interpretation, this is just $\neg p$. On the other hand, the assumption that we have a proof of $\neg p$ leads, by hypothesis, to a contradiction as well: $\neg p \to \bot$, that is, $\neg\neg p$. But as it was also assumed that p is decidable, from $\neg\neg p$ follows p. So in the case of both p and $\neg p$, the assumption that we have a proof of it leads to a contradiction and from there, in the proof interpretation, to a proof of $\neg p$ in the one case and of p in the other, deciding the undecidable proposition.

The argument does not show that, for any proposition p, the creating subject will at some stage decide p. All that can be said is: it is impossible that the subject will never decide p, for then p would be an absolutely undecidable proposition. On a classical conception of truth these are equivalents, but on the intuitionistic conception they are not.

Brouwer never published the argument; the Dutch intuitionist Dirk van Dalen suspects that he didn't find it important enough, and adds that the fact that Brouwer had this argument explains why he never searched for an absolutely undecidable proposition [46, p.174n.a].[18]

Brouwer did, however, exploit the proof interpretation to show that various classically valid propositions are as yet not intuitionistically acceptable. Our final example of his dealings with logic illustrates his technique.

Consider Goldbach's conjecture: every even number greater than or equal to 4 is the sum of two primes.[19] Expressed semi-formally, this is

$$\forall x \in \mathbb{N}(2x + 4 \text{ is the sum of two primes}) \tag{GC}$$

($\mathbb{N}$ indicates the natural numbers; later on, we will also see $\mathbb{Q}$ for the rational numbers, and $\mathbb{R}$ for the real numbers.) Let us note first that at the moment of writing, GC has been neither proved nor disproved, and on the proof interpretation of logic we have no right to claim $GC \vee \neg GC$. GC therefore presents a weak counterexample to the principle of the excluded middle.

More can be done. Define a sequence of rational numbers $a(n)$ as follows:

$$a(n) = \begin{cases} (-\frac{1}{2})^n & \text{if for all } j \leq n,\ 2j + 4 \text{ is the sum of two primes} \\ (-\frac{1}{2})^k & \text{if for some } k \leq n,\ 2k + 4 \text{ is not the sum of two primes} \end{cases}$$

We can always decide which case we are in; the idea is that as long as GC limited to $0, \ldots, n$ is true (the first clause), the $a(n)$ oscillate around 0 and become ever

smaller:
$$1, -\frac{1}{2}, \frac{1}{4}, -\frac{1}{8}, \ldots$$
but as soon as we hit upon a natural number k such that the even number $2k+4$ is not the sum of two primes, then $a(n)$ becomes constant (the second clause):
$$1, -\frac{1}{2}, \frac{1}{4}, -\frac{1}{8}, \ldots, (-\frac{1}{2})^k, (-\frac{1}{2})^k, (-\frac{1}{2})^k, \ldots$$
The sequence of the $a(n)$ satisfies the Cauchy condition, as for every n, any two members of the sequence after $a(n)$ lie within $(\frac{1}{2})^n$ of each other.[20] Therefore, the sequence determines a real number α. Note that α is defined by an algorithm, and does not depend on any intuitionistic idiosyncrasy; in the chapter on creating subject arguments, we will see counterexamples based on real numbers that are not defined by an algorithm.

If we find a counterexample to GC, then $\alpha = (-\frac{1}{2})^k$ for some k; if we never find such a k—and the only way to come to know this is to prove GC—then the $a(n)$ converge to 0 and $\alpha = 0$. As I am writing this, it has been verified that all even numbers from 4 to $4 \cdot 10^{14}$ are the sum of two primes.[21] Incredibly large as this range is, the result does not yet prove Goldbach right, and it is a difficult question whether it can be taken to provide inductive evidence for the truth of the conjecture or not; what is certain is that until GC has been actually proved or disproved, we do not know whether $\alpha = 0$ or rather a small number close to 0 but different.

Brouwer called real numbers such as α pendulum numbers. Wittgenstein thought that a pendulum number couldn't be a real number (in both senses of the word 'real'), precisely because they are not comparable with the rationals, for example, of α we do not know $\alpha = 0 \lor \alpha \neq 0$; as Wittgenstein said,

> If, now, there are constructions that cannot be compared with rational numbers, then we have no right to find them a place among the rational numbers. They simply are not on the number line. [143, p.73]

But, as we will see in chapter 3, Brouwer defined a real number (a point on the continuum) by asking for just a convergent sequence; from that point of view, whether a real number can be compared with the rationals is another, secondary question. Brouwer accepts that not every convergent sequence generates a decimal expansion as just a fact about the real numbers. (And when Wittgenstein continues, 'In Brouwer it appears as if they were real numbers about which we merely did not *know* whether they were larger than, or smaller than, or equal to another rational number', he is in danger of falling victim to the idea that intuitionism is primarily an epistemic affair. See p.20 above.)

Here are three weak counterexamples based on the pendulum number α [24]:

1. We do not now have a proof of $\forall x \in \mathbb{R}(x = 0 \lor x \neq 0)$, because we cannot say yet $\alpha = 0 \lor \alpha \neq 0$: to do so, we need, according to the proof interpretation, a proof of one of the disjuncts. But as the Goldbach conjecture is still undecided, we do not have such a proof.

2. We do not now have a proof of $\forall x \in \mathbb{R}(x < 0 \lor x = 0 \lor x > 0)$, by similar reasoning;

3. We do not now have a proof of $\forall x \in \mathbb{R}(x \in \mathbb{Q} \lor x \notin \mathbb{Q})$, for to know that $\alpha \in \mathbb{Q}$ we have to know $m, n \in \mathbb{Z}$ such that $\alpha = \frac{m}{n}$, but we can't as long as we do not know the value of α.

These three weak counterexamples are situated in analysis (to be specific, the algorithmic or recursive part of analysis). They show that we have no reason to transfer certain classically valid principles to intuitionistic analysis. Of course these particular weak counterexamples no longer work as soon as GC is decided; but then they can be made dependent on another unsolved problem. As long as there are open problems, such counterexamples can be constructed.[22]

As we will see in chapters 4 and 5, in intuitionistic analysis one can even prove strong counterexamples—prove, that is, that certain classical principles lead to actual inconsistencies if imported into intuitionism. The third counterexample on the list, for instance, turns out to be an understatement, in that it can actually be shown that

$$\neg \forall x \in \mathbb{R}(x \in \mathbb{Q} \lor x \notin \mathbb{Q})$$

(for a reason that has little to do with pendulum numbers, and which will be explained in chapter 4).

However, the fact that in classical pure logic and arithmetic (as opposed to analysis) various principles are used to which there are intuitionistic weak counterexamples does not give intuitionistic pure logic and arithmetic any advantage as far as safety against inconsistencies is concerned. That it does not was demonstrated by Gödel (and, independently, by Gentzen) in 1933 [58]; the conclusion had been anticipated by Kolmogorov in 1925 [96]. First, Gödel defined the following translation ′ from classical predicate logic into intuitionistic predicate logic:

$$A' = \neg\neg A \text{ for atomic } A$$
$$(A \land B)' = A' \land B'$$
$$(A \lor B)' = A' \lor B'$$
$$(A \to B)' = A' \to B'$$
$$(\forall x A(x))' = \forall x A'(x)$$
$$(\exists x A(x))' = \neg \forall x \neg A'(x)$$

Then he showed that

$$\Gamma \vdash_c A \Leftrightarrow \Gamma' \vdash_i A'$$

where $\Gamma' = \{B' | B \in \Gamma\}$, and $\vdash_c$ and $\vdash_i$ denote derivation relations in formal systems for classical and intuitionistic predicate logic.

Classically, a sentence A and its translation A' are equivalent, $\vdash_c A \leftrightarrow A'$; from an intuitionistic point of view, however, disjunctions and existential statements will be weakened by the translation. Still, Gödel's result shows that, formally, classical predicate logic can be embedded into intuitionistic predicate logic.

Taking $A = \bot$ and noting that $\bot' = \bot$, it follows that classical predicate logic is consistent if and only if intuitionistic predicate logic is; so the philosophical advantages of intuitionistic over classical predicate logic must lie in its interpretation and not in its trustworthiness.

Moreover, Gödel showed that the same holds if to predicate logic one adds the axioms of Peano arithmetic. So for arithmetic too, the advantages of the intuitionistic version over the classical one must lie in its interpretation. This once again shows that intuitionistic arithmetic is stronger than finitism, for it is hardly plausible that classical arithmetic can be translated into a finitistic system [8].

Although Brouwer always considered classical logic of no value whatsoever in the creative enterprise of mathematics, later in life, when various spectacular theorems of classical metamathematics had been proved, he did come to see something good about it:

> Fortunately classical algebra of logic [i.e. Boole and so on] has its merits quite apart from the question of its applicability to mathematics. Not only as a formal image of the technique of common-sensical thinking has it reached a high degree of perfection, but also in itself, as an edifice of thought, it is a thing of exceptional harmony and beauty. Indeed, its successor, the sumptuous symbolic logic of the twentieth century which at present is continually raising the most captivating problems and making the most surprising and penetrating discoveries, likewise is for a great part cultivated for its own sake. [35, p.116]

Chapter 3

Choice sequences

In the 'second act of intuitionism', Brouwer recognized choice sequences as mathematical objects. On the one hand, these are not acceptable to classical mathematics; on the other, they are at the basis of Brouwer's analysis of the continuum.

Imagine that you have a collection of mathematical objects at your disposal, let's say the natural numbers. Pick out one of them, and note the result. Put it back into the collection, and choose again. You may choose a different one, or the same again. Note the result, and put it back. For example, perhaps you chose
$$12, 3$$
Making further choices, you may arrive at
$$12, 3, 81, 12, 221$$
and you can continue from there. A *choice sequence* is what you get if you think of the sequence we are making as potentially infinite. The two sequences given above are *initial segments* of the choice sequence. Initial segments are always finite. We cannot make an actually infinite number of choices, but we can always extend an initial segment by making a further choice. This potential infinity of the choice sequence we indicate by three dots. Let's call this choice sequence α:
$$\alpha = 12, 3, 81, 12, 221, \ldots$$
Although choice sequences are never complete, the subject can generate them in parallel, in zig-zag fashion: make a few choices for α, then for β, then for γ, turn back to α to extend it a bit further, and so on.

Brouwer used choice sequences to give a mathematical analysis of continua, such as those of space and time. We will look at the example of the spatial continuum of the straight line. To this purpose, we use choice sequences of rational intervals (pairs of rational numbers) instead of natural numbers.[23] A rational interval specifies a part of the continuum by saying what the lower and upper boundaries of that part are, where these boundaries have to be rational numbers. It can be shown that it means no loss of generality if one demands that at choice ν we choose a rational interval of the particular form

$$\lambda_\nu = \left[\frac{a}{2^{\nu-1}}, \frac{a+2}{2^{\nu-1}}\right]$$

Brouwer then defines a point or real number as follows:

> We ... consider an indefinitely proceedable sequence of *nested* λ-intervals $\lambda_{\nu_1}, \lambda_{\nu_2}, \lambda_{\nu_3}, \ldots$ which have the property that every $\lambda_{\nu_{i+1}}$ lies *strictly* inside its predecessor λ_{ν_i} $(i = 1, 2, \ldots)$. Then [according to the definition of λ-intervals] the length of the interval $\lambda_{\nu_{i+1}}$ at most equals half the length of λ_{ν_i}, and therefore the lengths of the intervals converge to 0 ... *We call such an indefinitely proceedable sequence of nested λ-intervals a point P or a real number P.* We must stress that for us the point P is the sequence
>
> $$\lambda_{\nu_1}, \lambda_{\nu_2}, \lambda_{\nu_3}, \ldots \quad (1))$$
>
> *itself*; not something like 'the limiting point to which according to classical conception the λ-intervals converge and which could according to this conception be defined as the unique accumulation point of midpoints of these intervals'.
>
> Every one of the λ-intervals (1) is therefore *part of* the point P. [38, p.69, original emphasis]

It is worth stressing that intuitionistically, the choice sequence, growing in time, itself is the real number. It would be incorrect, therefore, to say, as Hintikka does, 'One can according to [Brouwer] construct an infinite choice sequence of zeros and ones, but we do not thereby come to know what the real number is whose binary expansion one thereby obtains' [79, p.15]. On Brouwer's construal, one knows very well what that real number is, for it is the proceeding sequence itself. It is not the case that a choice sequence is a method to approximate a real number that lies in transcendent reality waiting to be reached by the subject.

In classical mathematics, there are alternative but equivalent ways to define real numbers (e.g., Dedekind, Cantor). What they have in common is that the continuum is analysed as an infinite set of discrete elements. It is an atomistic conception of the continuum. The atoms are the real numbers. They have an actually infinite decimal expansion. At any time, it is fixed what the n-th decimal in the expansion is, whether we know it or not. This is responsible for their discreteness. The real numbers are lying apart from one another.

However, as Husserl has described in his analyses of intuitive time, continua are not built up from atoms. For example, a moment in time is not a dimensionless point, but a little 'halo'. The same holds for space. A line is what Husserl [88, p.276] calls an 'extensive whole': it is a whole such that the relation between the whole and its parts is the same as between those parts and their parts. Every part of a continuum is itself a continuum. This means that if one keeps dividing a continuum, one never arrives at something that is not continuous, not even 'ideally' or 'in the limit'. As Brouwer put it in his dissertation from 1907,

> continuity and discreteness occur as inseparable complements, both having equal rights and being equally clear, it is impossible to avoid one of them as a primitive entity, trying to construe it from the other one, the latter being put forward as self-sufficient. [11, p.17]

The mutual irreducibility of the discrete and the continuous was recognized also by Aristotle, Leibniz, Kant, Brentano, and Weyl, among others. The intuitive continuum exhibits a *homogeneity* that cannot be captured set-theoretically [5, p.426n.2]. Around 1689, Leibniz wondered how to capture intuitive continuity mathematically, and wrote

> There are two labyrinths of the human mind, one concerning the composition of the continuum, and the other concerning the nature of freedom, and they arise from the same source, infinity. [102, p.95]

As far as we know, Brouwer never made an extensive study of Leibniz, but the solution to the question of mathematical modelling of continuity that he came up with depended precisely on the other notion that the Freiherr mentions, freedom. How?

Imagine that beside the choice sequence

$$\alpha = 12, 3, 81, 12, 221, \ldots$$

above, you also begun a choice sequence

$$\beta = 12, 3, 81, 12, 221, \ldots$$

We see that the initial segments of α and β are identical. Does this mean that the *choice sequences* α and β are also identical? We cannot say, as there is no fact of the matter. Nothing can be said about whether the two sequences will develop in the same way in the future. The choices made so far are the same, but they don't have to be in the future. The future of each sequence is still open, it is not fixed. It only depends on your free choices and is not already determined. Therefore, a sequence can not, at any stage, have (or lack) a certain property if that could not be demonstrated from the information available at that stage. It is choice sequences that Brouwer was thinking of when he wrote

> In intuitionist mathematics a mathematical entity is not necessarily predeterminate, and may, in its state of free growth, at some time acquire a property which it did not possess before. [35, p.114]

In particular, the principle of the excluded middle does not hold generally for statements about choice sequences. For example, we have no right to assume

$$\alpha = \beta \lor \alpha \neq \beta$$

Similarly, we have no right to assume that either there are infinitely many 2's in α, or there are not. This may be different in specific cases, of course: if you stipulate that all choices for α will from now on be 2, then the left disjunct can be affirmed.

For *points* in the sense of Brouwer's definition given above, this undecidability models the fact that a point on the continuum is not a dimensionless atom but a 'halo'. Thus, the intuitive continuity of the line is preserved.[24]

The main argument for analysis with choice sequences as opposed to classical set theory is therefore *not* based on a cardinality consideration, but on the mutual irreducibility of the notions of discreteness and continuity. A continuum cannot be built up from discrete elements, however many, for these leave gaps. See e.g. [50] or [3]. As Hermann Weyl put it, in the classical continuum of real numbers, the points are *exactly* as isolated from one another as the natural numbers [142, ch.2, section 6, fn.2].

In classical mathematics, real numbers defined as sequences (Cantor's method) and real numbers defined by 'cuts' that divide the rationals into those smaller than the real number and those equal to or greater than it (Dedekind's method) are equivalent. Intuitionistically, that is not the case, and the sequences prevail. The reason is that, for example, a pendulum number (see p.27) can be defined as a sequence but we cannot indicate how it cuts the rationals into two sets of the required sort.

Brouwer distinguished different types of choice sequence. The subject is free in its choices, and therefore also free to pose restrictions on them. For example, the subject may decide to let its choices be prescribed by an algorithm (as will be familiar from Kant, subordinating oneself to a rule may be a perfect expression of one's freedom, so it is not incoherent to call such a sequence a *choice* sequence). A sequence generated that way is called 'lawlike'. Lawlike sequences are necessary, without them it would be impossible to prove that there are real numbers such as 0, π, and $\sqrt{2}$!

Brouwer's constructivist predecessors (e.g. Poincaré, Borel) and indeed the early Brouwer did not see how construct a theory of real numbers that goes beyond the lawlike. Yet, sequences other than the lawlike are necessary, because laws, when made precise, are formulated in a specific language and therefore denumerable, whereas Cantor's diagonal method shows that the real numbers are not.

Sequences that are not lawlike are the answer. The subject may decide to forbid any restriction on the numbers it chooses. Then you get a 'lawless' sequence. The lawlike and the lawless sequences are extremes at the two ends of a spectrum. There are many possibilities in between. For example, if you add two lawless sequences elementwise, you get a sequence that is neither lawless (for it depends on two other ones) nor lawlike (for the sequences it depends on are lawless).

One may, like Markov and Bishop, settle for just lawlike sequences (defining 'lawlike' as 'recursive'), but, while practical, that also amounts to ducking the issue how to model the full continuum. Brouwer's achievement is to have found a way to analyse the continuum that does not let it fall apart into discrete elements (as extensional equality of choice sequences is not decidable), and is constructive to boot.

Restrictions can also be of higher order, i.e., restrictions can be subjected to restrictions. For example, the subject may constrain the generation of a choice sequence by not allowing any restrictions on the choices of the values. This is a second-order restriction: 'No first-order restrictions are allowed'. Of course, this defines exactly the lawless sequences. So even a lawless sequence is a sequence subject to a restriction; but one of second order, not first. (This may well have been the reason why Gödel suggested replacing the term 'free choice sequences' by 'lawless'.) In full generality, we can think of a choice sequence as a sequence of tuples

$$(n_i, R_1^i, R_2^i, \ldots, R_{k_i}^i)$$

where at stage i the subject chooses an object n_i and a finite number of restrictions of orders $1 \ldots k_i$. An individual choice sequence has all of its properties solely in virtue of the subject's decision to construct it in a particular way. For this reason, choice sequences are highly intensional objects.

Choice sequences have desirable properties if one wishes to model the intuitive continuum, but they come for a price, or at least, that is how it seems from a non-intuitionistic point of view. The objects of classical mathematics have their properties independently from us and are static. Choice sequences, in contrast, depend on the subject (who has to make the choices), and they change through time. They *come* into being, at the moment that the subject decides to create them, and with each further choice, they grow. This is the case even for lawlike sequences.

Because of this dependence on the subject and on time, some have considered choice sequences to be empirical objects, and hence as having no place in pure mathematics (Wittgenstein and Gödel come to mind). But Brouwer did not mean the empirical subject and empirical time; this will be elaborated in the chapter on intersubjectivity. As mentioned in chapter 1, from Brouwer's point of view, the possibility of choice sequences as mathematical objects is implicit in the *first* act of intuitionism.

Brouwer never gave up the primitive (i.e., irreducible) intuition of the continuum.[25] Doing so would have meant to reject the complementarity of continuity and discreteness. And one still needs the primitive intuition in order to explain what it is that is analysed with choice sequences. But it is true that after the introduction of choice sequences, Brouwer hardly ever discusses this complementarity. This is because together with choice sequences, he introduced the notion of a spread. It will be discussed in the next chapter; it is a means to collect choice sequences. In particular, mathematically the continuum can be captured by a spread. Now we can understand Heyting's explanation:

> From 1918 on Brouwer no longer mentions the continuum as a primitive notion. He can do without it because the spread defined above represents it completely, as far as its mathematical properties go. [76, p.84]

Even when choice sequences are philosophically advantageous, how can they ever be put to use? The problem seems to be this: if we want to apply a function to a choice sequence, or evaluate whether a predicate holds of it, a sequence will have to act as an argument, to which then a method is applied to calculate the function's output or a truth value. But we cannot construct the argument in its entirety, as a choice sequence always is an unfinished object. There will never be a moment, then, at which the argument is fully constructed and the subject can go on to apply the function or predicate to it.

In some cases it is obvious that not the whole choice sequence is needed, for example, if the function returns the 10th number in the sequence. But what about the general case? Brouwer found the answer: one never needs the whole sequence. Specifically, the weak continuity principle for numbers (WC-N) says that a total function from choice sequences to natural numbers never needs more input than an initial segment to produce its output; hence all choice sequences sharing this segment will yield the same value. In a formula:

$$\forall \alpha \exists x A(\alpha, x) \Rightarrow \forall \alpha \exists m \exists x \forall \beta [\bar{\beta} m = \bar{\alpha} m \rightarrow A(\beta, x)] \tag{WC-N}$$

where α and β range over choice sequences of natural numbers, m and x over natural numbers, and $\bar{\alpha} m$ stands for $\langle \alpha(0), \alpha(1), \ldots, \alpha(m-1) \rangle$, the initial segment of α of length m. The antecedent says that to each choice sequence α is related a natural number x; the consequent says that there is a natural number m such that any choice sequence β the first m choices of which are the same as in α is likewise related to the same x. Thus, sharing the first m values with α is a sufficient condition for any sequence β to be related to that x, and no other properties of β need be relied upon. One speaks of *weak* continuity as the principle only says something about each α individually (local continuity).[26]

Intuitionistically, the assignment of a function value to an argument requires a construction. It is clear that, when the argument is a choice sequence, two types of information about the argument are available to the subject. First, there is the initial segment of choices made so far. This is extensional information: it doesn't matter how the sequence is defined, only what choice is made at what place. Second, there is the set of restrictions that the subject may have imposed so far. This is intensional information: it depends on how the sequence is defined. Both pieces of information are finite; out of these, the function value has to be constructed. The weak continuity principle claims that, if the function is defined for all choice sequences, only the first type of information is needed.

Without a principle such as WC-N, choice sequences could hardly be more than curiosa. The principle has always been held plausible, and Brouwer used it freely, but he never gave a justification.[27]

Limited to the lawless sequences, the validity of WC-N is obvious: as there are no first-order restrictions, there simply is no information about the choices except for the values chosen so far. (A first-order restriction would give information about future choices, as it puts a constraint on them.) So any other sequence with the same initial segment, when used as an argument for A, must give the same result.

What about the universe of all choice sequences? One might try the following. Assume we have a proof of $\forall \alpha \exists x A(\alpha, x)$. That means that if we take a particular α, we can begin to construct a proof of $\exists x A(\alpha, x)$. When we are done, only finitely many values of α have been chosen, as proofs are completed in finite time. Therefore, for any β with the same initial segment we have $\exists x A(\beta, x)$.

The problem with this argument is that the possible presence of intensional information has been neglected. For example, suppose that of the sequence α four values have been chosen so far, but also, at the fourth step, a restriction has been posed that from now on α is constant. Then one can immediately say what the 100th value in α will be. However, only four values of α have been chosen, and it is certainly not the case that any β that begins with the same four values will also agree with α on the 100th position.

One could try to save the argument by allowing only numerical information about choice sequences in the construction of proofs. In effect, this is to treat all sequences as if they were lawless. But then the principle would be established only for the class of the lawless sequences, which is not what we asked for. We would like to justify the principle for the universe of all choice sequences. What is required is an argument to the effect that, even if one is allowed to use intensional information, just an initial segment would suffice.

One way to obtain a rigorous argument would be to derive WC-N formally, from a suitable set of axioms; another, to justify it directly as an axiom. For the latter approach, Kreisel's 'informal rigour' commends itself:

> The 'old-fashioned' idea is that one obtains rules and definitions by analyzing intuitive notions ... Informal rigour wants (i) to make this analysis as precise as possible ... and (ii) to extend this analysis, in particular not to leave undecided questions which can be decided by full use of evident properties of these intuitive notions. [99, pp.138–139]

The need for informal rigour has been stressed by Gödel [63] and by Kreisel [99, 100].

Thus, we will seek to obtain an axiom for choice sequences from studying the way they are *given* in intuition. In particular, I suggest that applying Husserl's concept of the noetic-noematic correlation [87, e.g., §93 and §98] is one way of being informally rigorous. This correlation is one between the way in which an object is given to us (the noema), and the acts in which that object is intended (the noesis). Applied to choice sequences, this concept of correlation gives rise to the following question: in what ways can the freedom that the subject enjoys in the process of generating a choice sequence be reflected in the properties of that sequence itself?

When trying to answer this question, we immediately arrive at the two limiting cases, i.e., the lawless and the lawlike sequences; these were already known. However, further reflection shows that, as the subject has the freedom to impose restrictions, it also has the freedom to lift them again. This freedom leads to a distinction between definitive restrictions and provisional restrictions; the latter being those for which the subject reserves the right to lift them later.

Unless the subject explicitly lifts a provisional restriction, it remains in effect at subsequent stages.

What is the informational content of a provisional restriction? If you know that I imposed a provisional restriction at some earlier stage, what more do you know that you should not have known if I had imposed no restriction? The extra information that a provisional restriction gives you consists in the following. If I tell you that I will not begin by lifting the restriction, then you do immediately know something about my next choice of a value, namely, that it has to respect this unlifted restriction. Had I imposed no restriction, then you would not have known this. (Dialogue in the context of choice sequences is used by Brouwer too, e.g. in a course in 1933 [37, p.17].)

There is in the literature a type of choice sequence that, in hindsight, can be interpreted in terms of the definitive-provisional distinction. This is the 'hesitant sequence' mentioned by Troelstra and van Dalen [134, p.208]:

> A hesitant sequence is a process of generating values such that at any stage we decide that henceforth we are going to conform to a law in determining future values, or, if we have not already decided to conform to a law at an earlier stage, we freely choose a new value ... The decision whether or not to conform to a law may stay open indefinitely.

Thus, a hesitant sequence is begun like a lawless sequence: the choice of the values is free. This means that we have put a second-order restriction to the effect that we will not pose any first-order restriction. What is special about a hesitant sequence is that at any stage we may drop this second-order restricion and introduce a definitive first-order restriction, namely, a law that prescribes our future choices. The second-order restriction, then, was not definitive. Hence we can say that a hesitant sequence is, from the outset, a provisionally lawless sequence.

Given this distinction between provisional and definitive restrictions, we obtain a justification for WC-N if we demand that A (in the definition of WC-N, above) refers to a choice sequence only through the graph of that sequence, i.e. only by direct reference to what value appears at what place. That satisfies for analysis (e.g. [38], [134]). What makes a justification of WC-N difficult is that it may well be that information other than the graph could be used in constructing an x such that $A(\alpha, x)$ holds, i.e. intensional information. As we saw, this circumstance can spoil potential arguments for WC-N. What one has to show in order to accept WC-N is that such other information is not essential.

But the restrictions cannot be essential, as they are not stable. A restriction on a choice sequence may be provisional, and therefore does not necessarily characterize the sequence at all future stages. If we have a proof of $A(\alpha, x)$, then this relation should hold forever; but a construction for x that depends on provisional restrictions cannot guarantee this. The restrictions can therefore not be depended on in a construction, on pain of possibly yielding different results at different stages. (Because of the condition on A, the presence (or absence) of provisional restrictions on α cannot be exploited in the definition of A.) This leaves only the initial segment as reliable information; which is exactly what WC-N says.

The argument works for any universe which allows for any choice sequence also its 'provisionalized' counterpart, i.e., a choice sequence with the same restrictions but all provisional. The universe of all sequences by definition satifies this condition. A choice sequence that has some definitive restrictions put on it, and its provisionalized counterpart, are intensionally different choice sequences; hence different choice sequences simpliciter, as the intensional aspects are part of the sequence just like its numerical values; this is brought out above by the rendering of a choice sequence as a sequence of tuples

$$(n_i, R_1^i, R_2^i, \ldots, R_{k_i}^i)$$

The present argument is an example of how, in intuitionism, the notion of process is taken into account (and therefore, that talk of doing so need not be 'a sham' as Kreisel has it [100, pp.510–511]), as well as of Husserl's conviction that phenomenology provides the basic axioms for the a priori sciences [80].

In intuitionistic logic, $\forall \alpha \exists x A(\alpha, x)$ means that we have a method to construct, for any α, an x such that $A(\alpha, x)$ holds. If this is indeed the case, the availability of the method can be made explicit: $\exists f \forall \alpha A(\alpha, f(\alpha))$ for some constructive function f. WC-N informs us that f needs only an initial segment of α of a certain length m to calculate x. We can assume, first, that f will assign the same x to extensions of that segment, as additional but not strictly necessary information should not change the function value. We can also assume that the subject can decide of any initial segment whether it is long enough for f to produce its output. Functions for which these two assumptions hold form a class K_0 (which can be defined inductively). Thus we get:

$$\forall \alpha \exists x A(\alpha, x) \Rightarrow \exists f \in K_0 \forall \alpha A(\alpha, f(\alpha)) \qquad \text{(C-N)}$$

When, in the following, we speak of 'the continuity principle', C-N is meant. C-N is a strenghtening of WC-N—it gives more information—but it is just the result of combining WC-N with insights into what it means to have a method to compute a value.

We will see the continuity principle play an important role in the next chapter, but here is how it can be used to prove that the choice sequences are not denumerable (at the same time this is an alternative to Cantor's diagonalization argument that the real numbers are not denumerable).

Suppose we have an enumeration of all choice sequences, such that to different choice sequences corresponds a different natural number. According to the continuity principle (or WC-N), the number corresponding to a particular choice sequence must be determinable from an initial segment of that sequence. But then any other sequence sharing that initial segment will be assigned the same number, even if the sequences diverge later on. As one can always create diverging sequences from the same initial segment, this means that such an enumeration as we supposed we had cannot exist. That, on the other hand, there is an injection from the natural numbers to choice sequences is easily seen:

simply map the number n to the choice sequence that consists only of choices n. Combining this with the impossibility of an enumeration of choice sequences, one concludes that there are more choice sequences than natural numbers [16, p.13].

Chapter 4

Brouwer's proof of the bar theorem

4.1 The theorem and its philosophical interest

A formulation of the bar theorem must be postponed until some basic concepts that figure in it have been introduced, but its place in intuitionism can already be indicated: it is the apotheosis of Brouwer's reconstruction of mathematics, both mathematically and philosophically. The bar theorem allowed him to go beyond other varieties of constructivism without betraying the principles of intuitionism. Responsible for this is mainly a corollary of the bar theorem, the fan theorem. Using that, Brouwer proved that all total functions on the continuum are continuous, and even uniformly so. The first result has the important consequence that in dealing with such functions, approximations will always work fine. The second is of vital importance for a satisfactory intuitionistic theory of integration (and, hence, of probability). It also helps considerably in finding intuitionistic counterparts to theorems in classical analysis. On the intuitionistic construals of the continuum and of logic the two continuity theorems are valid; on the respective classical construals, they are not. Yet classically they are valid for certain subclasses of functions, and the intuitionist may try to transform classical theorems that hold for such subclasses into intuitionistic theorems on all total functions. Even though intuitionistic mathematics is autonomous, the aim to find such counterparts is sound from an economical as well as from a missionary point of view.

Classically, the bar and fan theorems themselves are easily established; the fact that, having gone through the more complicated process of establishing them intuitionistically, Brouwer could prove theorems that are not classically valid, is accounted for by the presence of a third ingredient in his proofs, the continuity principle discussed in the previous chapter. It is this classically false principle that connects the bar theorem to the intuitionistic modelling of the continuum using choice sequences.

The philosophical value of the bar theorem lies both in its content—it makes the full continuum, which had always been intractable for constructivists, constructively manageable—and in the way its proof fully exploits the intuitionistic conceptions of truth as experienced truth and of proofs as mental constructions.

In this chapter we will go through one of Brouwer's proofs of the bar theorem. Although it is a bit technical, it is not particularly difficult, and moreover, we will find the notion of intentionality at the very heart of it. It comes into play in the deep reflection on the activity of the creating subject that the proof depends on. It was from this reflection that Brouwer's concept of a canonical proof emerged, which we discussed in chapter 2.

In the literature on intuitionism, the reader will find several versions of the proof, e.g. Kleene [95, 6.12], Heyting [75, 3.4], Dummett [49, 3.4]. They all provide different perspectives, and it pays to compare them. To facilitate reading Brouwer in the original, I will discuss one of his own presentations (and often use his own notation). The ones included in the anthologies edited by Mancosu (the proof from 1924 [19]) and van Heijenoort (the proof from 1927 [21]) are probably the most widely available.[28] They are different, although this is mostly a matter of cosmetics; I will discuss the 1927 version, and comment on the differences afterwards.[29]

Now the the key notions can be defined, and the theorem stated.

In general, mathematicians are not as interested in proving theorems about particular real numbers as they are in proving theorems about classes of real numbers and functions of real numbers. It will not do to collect choice sequences in a set in the Cantorian sense, because, intuitionistically, such sets can be no larger than denumerably infinite, which is too small for the continuum and many of its subsets. Rather, choice sequences are held together in a *spread* ('Menge', in Brouwer's original, somewhat confusing terminology, as it is the German word commonly used for Cantor's sets). Brouwer regretted that his definition suffers from a certain prolixity ([20, footnote 2]):

> A spread is a law on the basis of which, if repeated choices of arbitrary natural numbers are made, each of these choices either generates a definite sign series, with or without termination of the process, or brings about the inhibition of the process together with the definitive annihilation of its result; for every $n > 1$, after every unterminated and uninhibited sequence of $n - 1$ choices, at least one natural number can be specified that, if selected as the n-th number, does not bring about the inhibition of the process. Every sequence of sign series generated in this manner by an unlimited choice sequence (and hence generally not representable in a finished form) is called an element of the spread. We shall also speak of the common mode of formation of the elements of a spread M as, for short, the spread M. [20, pp.244–245], translation adapted from [67, p.453]

The last line of the definition indicates that a spread is a special kind of species.

Because, as we saw in chapter 1, Brouwer holds that mathematics is essentially languageless, in this definition 'sign' and 'sign series' are to be understood 'in the sense of *mental* symbols, consisting in previously obtained mathematical concepts' [28].

In a footnote to the above definition, Brouwer adds that the possibility of terminating the process at a certain point can be replaced by the possibility of having all choices from that point on generate 'nothing'. This 'nothing' is an empty sign series, but nevertheless an object, on a par with, for example, the empty set.

By way of explanation, this definition can be rephrased if we introduce the notions of a spread law and a correlation law.

The objects chosen in the choice sequences in the spread may be natural numbers but also any other kind of mathematical object (the condition being that the objects have been constructed prior to the spread). In the latter case, we conceptualize making a choice in a choice sequence in the spread as first choosing a natural number and then obtaining, via a mapping from the natural numbers to a fixed, countable species of objects of the other type, the object desired. This mapping is the correlation law.

For generality, Brouwer always assumes a correlation law; one obtains choice sequences of natural numbers simply by mapping each natural number to itself. Brouwer uses the term 'choice sequence' both for the original sequence of natural numbers and for what you get by applying the correlation law to it.

A spread law either admits a given finite segment of natural numbers, or inhibits it. There are three conditions on a spread law.

1. It should be decidable. That is, we should have a means to tell in finite time whether a given sequence $\langle a_0, a_1, \ldots a_n \rangle$ should be used in the construction. For example, we would not be sure how to proceed building the spread if our next step depended on an open problem of which we have no idea when it will be solved.

2. Of each admitted sequence, at least one immediate extension should be admitted as well. Each admissible sequence $\langle a_0, a_1, \ldots a_n \rangle$, must have an immediate extension $\langle a_0, a_1, \ldots a_n, a_{n+1} \rangle$ which is likewise admissible.

3. If a sequence is admitted, then so should all of its initial segments. This is a natural demand, as we use these sequences to bundle choice sequences, there should be no gaps or jumps. If $\langle a_0, a_1, \ldots a_n, a_{n+1} \rangle$ is admissible, then so is $\langle a_0, a_1, \ldots a_n \rangle$.

The admitted sequences form a growing tree, hence they are also known as nodes; that is, a node in the tree is identified with the path leading up to it. The root or top (I think of trees as growing downwards) of the tree is the empty sequence. Brouwer calls the paths through a tree, whether finite or infinite, its elements. By 'choice sequences' in the pregnant sense of the word, the infinite paths are meant.

Of a pair of nodes $\langle a_0, a_1, \ldots a_n \rangle$ and $\langle a_0, a_1, \ldots a_n, \ldots a_{n+k} \rangle$, we call the second a descendant of the first, and the first an ascendant of the second. If $k = 1$, we speak of an immediate descendant and an immediate ascendant.

The tree of admitted sequences may be called the underlying tree of the spread (Brouwer does not use this term, but speaks of 'the species of choice sequences upon which the spread is based'). The correlation law maps the elements of the underlying tree of natural numbers to the desired objects; like the underlying tree, the spread consists of nodes that form a tree.

To an admissible sequence, the correlation law assigns either an object, or 'nothing'. The latter option lets us simplify the definition of a spread by dropping the possibility of termination: one gets the same effect of a finite spread by always assigning, to each admissible sequence, 'nothing' from a certain point onwards.

An inadmissible sequence is inhibited. It will not play a role in the generation of the elements in the spread anymore, as the correlation law does not apply to such a sequence.

A special spread is the universal spread, the spread of choice sequences of natural numbers which inhibits no sequences, therefore admitting all.

As another example, consider the following spread J. Let $I_0, I_1, I_2, \ldots$ be an enumeration of the intervals of the continuum of the form

$$\left[\frac{a}{2^{k+1}}, \frac{a+2}{2^{k+1}} \right]$$

where $2 \leq a + 2 \leq 2^{k+1}$, so that the boundaries of these intervals are ≥ 0 and ≤ 1. (That they can be enumerated follows from the fact that each such interval is determined by a pair of natural numbers $\langle a, k \rangle$, and such pairs are enumerable.) The correlation law of J assigns to n the interval I_n. Let the spread law be: $\langle a_0, a_1, \ldots a_n, a_{n+1} \rangle$ is an admissible extension of $\langle a_0, a_1, \ldots a_n \rangle$ exactly if interval $I_{a_{n+1}}$ is properly contained in interval I_{a_n}. The elements of J are convergent sequences of intervals of $[0, 1]$. One can prove that J coincides with that interval; we will use J in our discussion of the fan theorem below.

Any node in a tree determines or dominates a particular subtree, namely, the subtree consisting of all paths that pass through that node. Equivalently, the subtree consists of the sequences that share the initial segment defining that node. We will call this subtree the subtree dominated by that node. A species of nodes determines a species of subtrees. As a spread is also a tree (in particular, it is a tree in which every node has at least one immediate descendant) we can also speak of subspreads.

The notion of a bar is defined as follows. If B is a bar for a spread M, this means that each of the infinite choice sequences in the underlying tree of the spread (call it U) has a finite initial segment which is an element of B:

$$\forall \alpha \in U \exists n (\bar{\alpha} n \in B)$$

A species of nodes is a bar, that is, if every infinite path though the tree has at least one node in common with it ('hits the bar'). A bar determines a subtree, namely the tree starting at the root of the underlying tree and ending in the nodes that have just hit the bar.

A first statement of the bar theorem as proved by Brouwer in 1927 would be: if B is a bar, then the species of nodes that have just reached B can be well-ordered. We will see a more precise statement in a moment, but this formulation suffices to give a clue why this theorem is useful.

Generally, the number of immediate successors of a node in a tree may be finite or infinite. A tree in which every node has only finitely many immediate successors is called a finitary tree or a fan. One also says that such a tree is finitely branching. The same goes for the underlying tree. The spread J that we just saw is in fact a fan. As we will see later, a corollary of the bar theorem is the fan theorem: if B is a bar for a fan, we can effectively determine a bound on the length of the paths to the bar. As Brouwer also showed how to represent the continuum by a fan, the fan theorem enables him to prove, given some suitable bar, theorems about the continuum by proving theorems about choice sequences of a certain bounded length. The latter certainly are much more managable than the continuum itself.

Brouwer seems to have proved the bar theorem solely for the purpose of establishing this corollary. From a classical point of view, the fan theorem is the contraposition of König's lemma, which was proved later: 'If a fan contains infinitely many nodes, it contains an infinite path'. But intuitionistically, König's lemma is not valid, so it cannot be used to obtain the fan theorem. The problem with the lemma is that it doesn't enable one actually to construct an infinite path through the fan. I will come back to the fan theorem and its relation to König's lemma later.

In order to give a more precise statement of the bar theorem, we need the notion of a thin bar, and make explicit a condition on B.

A thin bar is a bar that contains no more elements than necessary to be a bar:

$$b \in B \wedge a < b \to a \notin B$$

where a and b are variables for elements, and $a < b$ means 'b is an extension of a'. That is, a thin bar never contains a pair of nodes one of which is a descendant of the other. With respect to its property of being a bar, such descendants are superfluous. (Brouwer did not use the term 'thin bar' in print before 1954 [34]).

The condition is that the bar B should be decidable, that is, of any node we should be able to tell in finite time whether it belongs to the bar or not. The condition of decidability is not explicit in Brouwer's proofs of 1924 and 1927, but it is essential, as Kleene has shown; we will see a version of his argument in the comments on the proof of the bar theorem below. If one thinks of bars that are implicitly determined by the continuity principle, as Brouwer does in the two proofs mentioned, this condition is surely fulfilled. His point of departure is that of a spread M and a function that assigns to each element of M a natural number β. The continuity principle then says that for every sequence a number n can be found such that you need only the first n choices in the sequence to calculate the number β that the function assigns to it. Given an initial segment of a choice sequence—which corresponds to a node in the tree—determine n for that sequence; the segment belongs to the bar exactly if its length is equal to or greater than n, and this we can decide.

The bar theorem can now be stated as: if B is a decidable bar, then it contains a well-ordered thin bar.

So far, I have not said how the notion of well-ordering is defined in intuitionistic mathematics. An example will show that it cannot be the classical definition.

In the classical definition, a set is well-ordered if it is ordered and every non-empty subset has a first element. That every set can be well-ordered in this sense is implied by the axiom of choice. But that axiom does not hold in intuitionistic mathematics, for it does not tell you how to construct that first element. Here is an example of a species which can intuitionistically be shown non-empty, but of which we have yet no construction for an element. Let p be an as yet undecided proposition, say, Goldbach's conjecture that every even number is the sum of two odd primes. Now define the species A as follows:

$$x \in A \equiv (x = 0 \land p) \lor (x = 1 \land \neg p)$$

It is easy to see that A cannot be empty. Assume A contained no elements. On that assumption, both the condition for the inclusion of 0 and the condition for the inclusion of 1 must have failed. Then both p and $\neg p$ must be false, which is to say, $\neg p \land \neg \neg p$ is true. But that is a contradiction, so the assumption that A is empty must be false.

It is also easy to see that A cannot contain any element other than 0 or 1, as such an element would simply fail both conditions. So if x is an element of A, then it must be 0 or 1. It follows, therefore, that A is a subspecies of, for example, the species $\{0, 1, 2\}$.

However, we cannot indicate an element of A. To do so requires that we have established p or $\neg p$, which, by hypothesis, we have not.

All this means that there is a non-empty subspecies of $\{0, 1, 2\}$ of which we cannot say (now) that it has an element, let alone a first element, which would be required by a classical well-ordering. If we adopt that definition of a well-ordering in intuitionism, then the species $\{0, 1, 2\}$ would not be well-ordered.

Hence Brouwer had to resort to another definition of the notion. For this, he reached back to Cantor's original suggestion from 1883 (the now usual classical definition was a later suggestion of his) and defined well-ordering by induction. According to this definition, a species is well-ordered if it can be generated inductively, as follows:

Induction basis

> Any one-element species A is well-ordered. Brouwer calls such a species a primitive species.

Induction step

(a) Generating operation of the first kind
If $A_0, \ldots, A_n$ are a positive, finite number of disjunct well-ordered species, then their ordered sum is a well-ordered species. The 'ordered sum' of the A_i is their union, where each species remains ordered in its original way, but the clause is added that, if $j < k$, each element of A_j precedes each element of A_k: $a \prec b$ for $a \in A_j, b \in A_k$.

(b) Generating operation of the second kind
If $A_0, A_1, A_2, \ldots$ is a denumerable sequence—hence, on the intuitionistic understanding of infinity, given by a construction method—of well-ordered species, then their infinite ordered sum is also a well-ordered species. Here, $a \prec b$ is defined in the same way as in the generating operation of the first kind.

It is easily shown that every well-ordered species has a first element (in the intuitionistic sense, i.e., we can exhibit it), and that every element in a well-ordered species either has an immediate successor or is the last element. Together these properties ensure that for a well-ordered species we always have an effective method to run through its elements. Hence every well-ordered species is decidable, i.e., for any well-ordered species we have a method to tell whether a given element belongs to it or not.

Moreover, from this definition it is easily proved (by induction) that of every well-ordered species it can be indicated either that it is finite or that it is denumerably infinite.

For reasons that will become clear later, it is convenient to have the option of labelling the elements in a well-ordering either 'full' or 'null'. There is no intrinsic connection between an element and its label; the labelling depends on the particular use one wants to make of such a well-ordering. In our case, the labelling will help to distinguish admissible sequences from certain unadmissible ones.

We can now verify that $\{0, 1, 2\}$ is a well-ordered species according to this new definition. The induction basis says that every one-element species is well-ordered, and accordingly, $\{0\}$, $\{1\}$ and $\{2\}$ each are well-ordered. So by the first induction step, their ordered sum is also a well-ordered species. This construction is not unique: one might also first add $\{0\}$ and $\{1\}$, and then, again by induction step (a), add $\{0, 1\}$ and $\{2\}$. The order relations are the same in both cases. Note that species such as A, which we used above to show that not every non-empty subspecies of $\{0, 1, 2\}$ has a first element, need not bother us anymore. In the new definition, that no longer is the defining characteristic of a well-ordering.

Of course, if we somehow have an immediate view of all the nodes in a thin bar, then we can well-order it by sight. But such an overview is, but in the simplest of cases, out of the question, either because the bar contains a large and perhaps even infinite number of nodes, or because the proof that all infinite paths through a node of the underlying tree have an initial segment in the bar is complicated enough to leave it opaque what the species of these initial segments will look like; and often because of both. The whole point of the bar theorem is that in spite of this, it can still be shown that the thin bar can be well-ordered.

Here is a simple-minded attempt at a proof of the bar theorem. Certainly the infinite species of finite sequences of natural numbers, call it μ, can be well-ordered. For example, one can verify that the following rule will do. Let $a \prec b$ whenever a is shorter than b, and if a and b are of equal length, order them according to smallest first differing number: e.g., $\langle 1, 2, 3, 4 \rangle \prec \langle 1, 2, 4, 3 \rangle$. The first element in the whole species will be the empty sequence $\langle \rangle$. By hypothesis, the predicate 'm is in the bar', defined on μ, is decidable. Then so is the predicate 'm is in the thin bar', as it is then decidable for a given m in the bar whether any of its ascendants is too. This second predicate defines a subspecies μ_1 of μ; and we know that μ is well-ordered. Doesn't this prove the bar theorem?

It does not. We do not know now that μ_1 is also well-ordered. For one thing, it is a property of well-ordered species that we can determine either that it is finite or that it is infinite, but of μ_1 we cannot, in any case not yet. The knowledge that a given predicate defined on an infinite well-ordered species is decidable does not by itself give us a construction method for the species of elements for which that predicate holds. One way of looking at it is that the knowledge that the predicate provides when it holds is too local to derive something global from it. What is called for, then, is a deeper consideration of the nature of bars, so as to find a principle that somehow unifies the elements that make up a bar and from which a construction method for the thin bar can be derived. Thinking things through, Brouwer arrived at a method of induction, and moreover, an induction that does not work its way from the root of the tree to the thin bar, but from the thin bar to the root. Let us now see how this works.

4.2 Brouwer's proof

Brouwer's strategy is to divide the proof of the bar theorem,

> if B is a decidable bar, then it contains a well-ordered thin bar

into two parts:

1. Show that any proof of the antecedent, 'B is a decidable bar', can itself be rendered as a certain well-ordered species;

2. Show how, given this well-ordered species, one constructs a well-ordered thin bar, thus proving the consequent.

In intuitionistic proofs of implications, one usually doesn't need much more information about a proof of the antecedent beyond the fact that, in the case of a conjunction for example, one indeed has a proof of each conjunct. In the proof of the bar theorem, however, Brouwer analyses what a proof of the antecedent could be like in great detail.

4.2.1 Part 1

What information is available to us to prove that B is a (decidable) bar? First of all the spread M, and in particular, its underlying tree. The elements of the underlying tree are infinitely proceeding choice sequences of natural numbers. In the proof of the bar theorem we might as well work with initial segments of these elements, precisely because the nodes that we want to well-order are all in the bar. The species of initial segments of choice sequences of natural numbers is the species μ that we saw earlier. The elements of μ can be divided into two species: those that are admissible in M and those that are not admissible (the latter species might be empty, i.e., in the case of the universal spread). The elements of the bar B will all be in the first species.

Brouwer defines μ_1 to be the thin bar contained in B. μ_1 is the species of those elements of μ such that they are in B and their presence in B is not redundant, because they have no proper initial segment that is also in B. Every sequence that hits B also hits μ_1. We saw that B, as it is defined on the basis of the continuity principle, is a decidable bar; therefore, so is μ_1.

An element of μ is called *secured* (relative to the spread M) when we are sure of its status with respect to the thin bar μ_1: that is, when we either know that it has an initial segment in μ_1, or that it never will, because it is inhibited. Thus we can split the species μ in two, namely, into the species τ of secured elements (relative to M), and the species σ of unsecured elements (relative to M), that is, of the elmentents that are admissible but that have not yet hit the bar.

To have a proof that B is a thin bar means that, in particular, we have a proof h that shows that, for any element of σ, any infinite sequence α that is nowhere inhibited and of which this element is an initial segment will at some point n have hit B:

$$\forall \alpha \in M \exists n (\bar{\alpha} n \in B)$$

In accordance with the intuitionistic interpretation of the logical constants, any proof h of this statement supplies us with a method to construct, for a given α in the spread, this number n. The method specified by a particular h need not be the most efficient one, and even if it is, it may be still quite complex. Brouwer imagines possibilities such as the following:

> The algorithm in question may indicate the calculation of a maximal order n_1 at which will appear a finite method of calculation of a further maximal order n_2 at which will appear a finite method of calculation of a further maximal order n_3 at which will appear a finite method of calculation of a further maximal order n_4 at which the postulated node of intersection must have been passed.

'Much higher degrees of complication are thinkable,' he adds. As mentioned earlier, there can be a huge gap between having a proof that there is a bar and knowing exactly what the bar looks like.

We saw that in the setting in which Brouwer proves the bar theorem we have a spread M and a function or algorithm that assigns to every choice sequence in M a natural number β. Because of the continuity principle, this implicitly defines a thin bar μ_1 in the underlying tree. A sufficient condition for a node in M to have the property that any choice sequence passing through it will be assigned the same number β is that this node, or an ascendant of it, was obtained by the correlation law from a node in μ_1. But this is not a necessary condition: perhaps one can find, once a sufficient number of such assignments of numbers β to choice sequences have been determined, a node above the bar (i.e., in σ) such that its correlated node in M also has that property. The situation, when it occurs, is accounted for by the fact that the algorithm used to calculate β may not be clever enough to extract this number from shorter segments [21, pp.459–460]. (Under certain conditions, it is in fact necessary to put off the assignment until later [95, p.71].)

Of course, whether a given thin bar could have been placed higher up in the tree if we had a different algorithm does not influence the fact that any admissible sequence that passes through a node $\alpha(n)$ in the given thin bar is secured. In the presence of a proof h, an element of σ is therefore called 'securable'. (An element of σ cannot be inhibited altogether, for then the element would already have been in τ.) To say that there is a bar in a tree and to say that the root of that tree is securable are equivalent.

The essential statement Brouwer wants to prove is in paragraph 4 of §2: 'We now assert that every element $F_{sn_1...n_r}$ of σ possesses the *well-ordering property*.' (Brouwer uses the notation $F_{sn_1...n_r}$ for the element $\langle s, n_1, \ldots, n_r \rangle$ of σ.)

What Brouwer means by this is, essentially, that the thin bar of the subtree dominated by $F_{sn_1...n_r}$, that is, the thin bar that bars exactly those sequences that share the initial segment $F_{sn_1...n_r}$, admits of a well-ordered construction. Once this claim has been proved, it can then be instantiated for the subtree dominated by the root node, which is just the whole tree, barred by the whole thin bar.

Let us now take a look at Brouwer's own, precise definition of the well-ordering property of $F_{sn_1...n_r}$, in which also the spread M is taken into account. Consider the following two species. (See figure 4.1.)

- The subspread (after all, a species defined on a spread) $M_{sn_1...n_r}$ of M determined by $F_{sn_1...n_r}$. This subspread consists of all the infinite elements of M that share the initial segment obtained by successively applying the correlation law to the initial segments of $F_{sn_1...n_r}$ (i.e., first to F_s, then F_{sn_1}, then $F_{sn_1n_2}$, and so on).

- The species of subspreads M_α, where α is an extension of $sn_1 \ldots n_r$ such that F_α hits the thin bar but does not go beyond it. In other words, an M_α is a subspread of M determined by an F_α, where F_α is a descendant of $F_{sn_1...n_r}$ and is an element of μ_1. A species of such F_α defines a little thin bar, namely, that part of the whole thin bar which is responsible for barring the sequences with initial segment $F_{sn_1...n_r}$.

Clearly, the union of all M_α (the union of all the elements of the second species) is identical to $M_{sn_1...n_r}$ (the first species). In Brouwer's terms, the first species

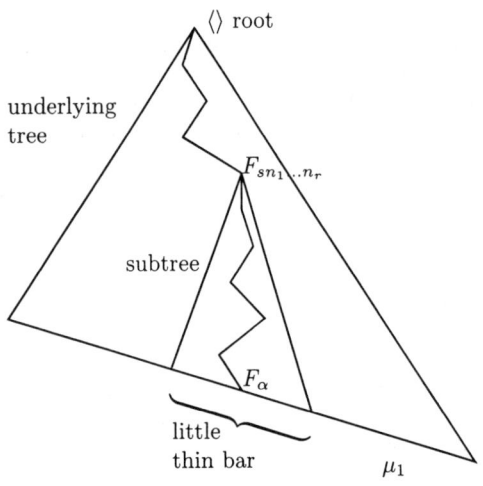

Figure 4.1: Little thin bar determined by $F_{sn_1...n_r}$

splits into the second species.

Now Brouwer defines the claim that $F_{sn_1...n_r}$ has the well-ordering property as the claim that the second species, the species of subspreads M_α, is similar to the species of full elements of a well-ordered species $T_{sn_1...n_r}$ (as we will see, the construction of this species T brings with it that T will contain null elements as well). It is claimed, that is, that we can construct a one-one relation between these two species that leaves the ordering relations invariant. In effect this means that the species of subspreads M_α can be well-ordered: first construct $T_{sn_1...n_r}$ and then use the one-one relation. As to each M_α corresponds F_α, this also yields a well-ordering of the F_α.

As mentioned, the aim is to show that the root of the whole tree has the well-ordering property. In that case, the corresponding F_α together make up the whole thin bar, because now α is any path reaching the thin bar from the root. Moreover, we can then think of T as a well-ordered construction of the whole thin bar.

Incidentally, Brouwer does not have the empty node as the root of the whole tree; instead, he proves the result for trees with arbitrary non-empty top, and the bars of all these trees taken together form the whole thin bar μ_1. But it is convenient to add all these trees together (in a generating operation of the second kind) with the empty node as top. As a matter of notation, F_s then is not, as in Brouwer, the one-number sequence $\langle s \rangle$, but the empty sequence $\langle \rangle$, and we will take $F_{sn_1...n_r}$ to refer to the element $\langle n_1, \ldots, n_r \rangle$ of σ.

If you think things through intuitionistically, Brouwer claims in footnote 7 of the 1927 paper, then you can actually see that the root has the well-ordering property, and no further proof is needed:

When carefully considered from the intuitionistic point of view, this securability is seen to be nothing but the property defined by the stipulation that it shall hold for every element of μ_1 and for every inhibited element of μ, and that it shall hold for an arbitrary $F_{sn_1...n_r}$ as soon as it is satisfied, for every ν, for $F_{sn_1...n_r\nu}$. This remark immediately implies the well-ordering property for an arbitrary $F_{sn_1...n_r}$.

The well-ordering property follows immediately, as the stipulations defining securability translate immediately to the induction clauses for one-element species and the second generating operation.

It has been questioned whether Brouwer's full proof of the bar theorem really is more evident than the principle formulated in this footnote; I will come back to that issue in the comments on Brouwer's proof below. But what can be said now is that the full proof certainly is more fundamental in the sense that it shows a finer-grained constructivism, turning, as we will see, on the issue what exactly a mental proof is.[30] This must be why Brouwer continues the footnote by saying

> The proof carried out in the text for the latter property, however, seems to me to be of interest nevertheless on account of the propositions contained in its elaboration.

In chapter 2 it was explained that proofs can always be thought of as consisting of just immediate facts and elementary inferences; proofs have a canonical form. We now see that these canonical forms are well-ordered trees. The immediate facts correspond to null elements as they are considered to be 0-step inferences. Elementary inferences correspond to generating operations of the first kind if they have a finite number of premises, and to operations of the second kind if they have infinitely many premises. A canonical form makes fully explicit the intentional structure of a proof.

Brouwer's intentional analysis of proofs of securability led him to the following conclusions. Any proof of a node's securability must turn on the relations between the various elements of the underlying tree, and these relations can be decomposed into basic relations that relate an element $F_{mm_1...m_g}$ to its immediate ascendant and to one or more of its immediate descendants $F_{mm_1...m_g m_{g+1}}$. In a proof in which only these basic relations play a role, these relations are established by elementary inferences. According to Brouwer, these are:

1. Immediate facts or 0-step inferences which show the securability of a secured element. Brouwer didn't give these a name. If an element is secured because it is in the bar, Kleene called the 0-step proof of this an η-inference (pronounced 'eta-inference'); Dummett follows this. The other possibility, that the element is secured because it is inhibited, does not occur in Kleene's proof because he proves the bar theorem for just the universal spread (which means no loss of generality, as any spread can be embedded in it).

2. ζ-inferences (pronounced 'zeta-inferences'). From the securability of $F_{mm_1...m_{g-1}}$, conclude the securability of $F_{mm_1...m_g}$. (Rationale: if all paths through a node hit the bar, then surely a path through one of that node's immediate descendants hits the bar.)

3. F-inferences.[31] From the securability of $F_{mm_1...m_g\nu}$ for all ν, conclude the securability of $F_{mm_1...m_g}$. (Rationale: if all paths through any of a node's immediate descendants hit the bar, then all paths through that node hit the bar.) This inference has infinitely many premises. It therefore depends on the existence of a construction method for the species of its premises.

Canonical proofs are built out of these elementary inferences; and the way they are combined makes such a proof a well-ordered species. The 0-step-inferences are the primitive species; ζ-inferences correspond to the generating operation of the first kind; and F-inferences to that of the second kind. That these proofs have a well-ordered structure is at the basis of Brouwer's proof of the bar theorem.

A canonical proof for the securability of the element $F_{sn_1...n_r}$ is indicated by, for example, $k_{sn_1...n_r}$.

Canonical proofs need not be as efficient as possible. They may contain detours and redundancies by proving securability of a given node more than once. We will see that this does not influence the proof of the bar theorem in any essential way.

4.2.2 Part 2

The idea behind the second part is that we first construct proofs of the bar theorem for little bars near the bottom of the tree, and then show that if such proofs for small bars are combined, we obtain a proof of the bar theorem for a larger subtree. Joining ever larger subtrees in this way finally brings one back to the top of the whole tree, yielding a proof of the bar theorem. Thus, the proof is by induction on proofs for subtrees; but it differs from more common forms of induction in two ways.

First, it is induction in the reverse direction from the usual: it proceeds from the bottom of the tree to the top ('backward', [95, p.65]).

Second, this induction is transfinite because, as we will see, the number of premises in the induction step (corresponding to the number of subtrees involved in the step upwards in the tree) is infinite.

The data available to us to carry out the proof that each element of σ has the well-ordering property are μ_1, the inhibited sequences, and the canonical proofs.

In order to be able to make use of the canonical proofs, Brouwer defines two properties on them, based on the following circumstances.

- A canonical proof $k_{sn_1...n_r}$ is a well-ordered species; it is built up inductively from subspecies which are themselves proofs. These are called the constructive underspecies of the species, and they include as special case the species itself. Each of these constructive underspecies is a proof ascertaining the securability of a particular element.

- Because of the first circumstance, one can construct from $k_{sn_1...n_r}$ the well-ordered species $f_{sn_1...n_r}$ of the elements of σ whose securability is established in the course of it. This species in particular contains $F_{sn_1...n_r}$ itself.

The two properties are:

the well-ordering property From the already defined well-ordering property for elements, one for canonical proofs is derived. A constructional underspecies u of $k_{sn_1...n_r}$ (that is, one of the subproofs out of which $k_{sn_1...n_r}$ is built) has the well-ordering property for canonical proofs if every element σ of f_u (that is, every element of which the securability is established in the course of u) has the well-ordering property for elements.

the preservation property[32] A constructional underspecies u of $k_{sn_1...n_r}$ has the preservation property if the following holds: if every element of $f_{sn_1...n_r}$ of which the securability functions as a premise in u has the well-ordering property, then every element of $f_{sn_1...n_r}$ of which the securability is derived in the course of u also has the well-ordering property. It is the preservation property that guarantees that, if we join proofs of the bar theorem for little bars, we get a proof of the bar theorem for the bar that combines these little bars.

In Brouwer's text, the whole proof that every element $F_{sn_1...n_r}$ of σ has the well-ordering property passes by in one short paragraph. It consists of three steps:

1. The preservation property holds for $k_{sn_1...n_r}$

2. Therefore, the well-ordering property (for proofs) holds for $k_{sn_1...n_r}$

3. Therefore, the well-ordering property (for elements) holds for $F_{sn_1...n_r}$

One sees from this proof that the well-ordering property of a node rides pickaback on the preservation property of canonical proofs of its securability. That a node has a certain property is derived here from a property of certain proofs; this move is typical for intuitionism. Let's go through these three steps now.

1. The preservation property holds for $k_{sn_1...n_r}$ By induction along the construction of $k_{sn_1...n_r}$ (which, after all, is a well-ordered species):

   induction basis

   The primitive species in a canonical proof are the 0-step-inferences, proving the securability of a secured element. These are 0-step proofs and have 0 premises. So, vacuously, a 0-step-inference preserves the well-ordering property.

   induction step

   (a) F-inference
   As this elementary inference has infinitely many premises, this is where we will use transfinite induction. The premises are canonical proofs of the securability of nodes $F_{mm_1...m_g\nu}$, for all ν. What we have to prove is that, if each of these nodes has the well-ordering property, so has the the node of which the F-inference in question proves the securability, $F_{mm_1...m_g}$; this node is the top of the subtree in which the subtrees dominated by the nodes in the premise are combined. Assume that the nodes $F_{mm_1...m_g\nu}$ have the well-ordering property for every ν. Then to each corresponds a well-ordered species of nodes $T_{mm_1...m_g\nu}$ forming a little thin bar. These species are all disjoint, as the initial segments $\langle m, m_1, \ldots m_g\nu \rangle$ of the nodes in different species will differ in their value for ν. But then they can be added in a generating operation of the second kind, giving the well-ordered species $T_{mm_1...m_g}$, which shows that $F_{mm_1...m_g}$ has the well-ordering property.

   (b) ζ-inference
   Its premise is a canonical proof of the securability of $F_{mm_1...m_{g-1}}$. Assume that $F_{mm_1...m_{g-1}}$ has the well-ordering property. Then to this node corresponds a well-ordered species of nodes $T_{mm_1...m_{g-1}}$ forming a little thin bar. But a decidable subspecies of this one is that of all elements having initial segment $F_{mm_1...m_g}$; then this subspecies is $T_{mm_1...m_g}$, establishing that $F_{mm_1...m_g}$ has the well-ordering property.

   We see that a canonical proof $k_{sn_1...n_r}$ always has the preservation property.

2. Therefore, the well-ordering property holds for $k_{sn_1...n_r}$

   That $k_{sn_1...n_r}$ has the preservation property implies that it has the well-ordering property, as follows. $k_{sn_1...n_r}$ as a whole has as given only the securability of the elements in μ_1 and the inhibited sequences. In other words, the well-ordered construction of $k_{sn_1...n_r}$ has to start from proofs that are null elements, corresponding to the fact that secured elements

(elements of τ, i.e., in the bar or inhibited) are trivially securable (0-step proof). These are its primitive species. A canonical proof determines a species of elements, namely the species of those elements of which it establishes their securability. In the case of a null proof, this species has exactly one element, and is therefore well-ordered by definition. By preservation, $k_{sn_1...n_r}$, built up starting from these primitive species, has the well-ordering property.

3. Therefore, the well-ordering property holds for $F_{sn_1...n_r}$

The fact that the well-ordering property (for proofs) holds for $k_{sn_1...n_r}$ means that, in particular, the element of σ of which this proof as a whole establishes the securability, $F_{sn_1...n_r}$, has the well-ordering property (for elements).

This enables us to conclude that the well-ordering property holds for the root of the tree, $\langle\rangle$: $F_{sn_1...n_r}$ was arbitrarily chosen from the nodes in σ, so we are allowed to infer that *every* element of σ has the well-ordering property. Instantiating that conclusion for the root of the tree, we conclude that the thin bar of the subtree with the root as top, that is, the thin bar of the whole tree, admits of a well-ordered construction. This proves the bar theorem.

We will now have a closer look at how this proof specifies the construction, for an arbitrary element $F_{sn_1...n_r}$ of σ, of $T_{sn_1...n_r}$.

The species T is constructed using generating operations of the second kind. This operation corresponds, as Brouwer puts it in the fourth paragraph of §2, 'to the inversion of the continuation, by a new free choice, of a certain finite initial segment of choices that is uninhibited for M'. By this he refers to the fact that we are building in the opposite direction from the usual, so that now species corresponding to descendants are constructed before the species corresponding to their immediate ascendant. The well-ordered species $T_{sn_1...n_r\nu}$ to be added in the infinite sum with $T_{sn_1...n_r}$ as top are now determined as follows:

- If $F_{sn_1...n_r\nu}$ is inadmissible, we take a primitive species consisting of ν as a null element.

- If $F_{sn_1...n_r\nu}$ is admissible and moreover is an element of μ_1, we take a primitive species consisting of ν as a full element.

- In the remaining case, where $F_{sn_1...n_r\nu}$ is admissible but is not an element of μ_1, that is, is unsecured, we appeal to our backward induction hypothesis, by which we already have a well-ordering $T_{sn_1...n_r\nu}$ of the little bar of the subtree dominated by $F_{sn_1...n_r\nu}$; this $T_{sn_1...n_r\nu}$ will be the summand.

One sees how the construction of the well-ordering depends on the fact that μ_1 is a decidable species, which in turn was guaranteed by the decidability of the bar.

The primitive species of $T_{sn_1...n_r}$ that have been predicated full correspond to the subspreads of M determined by the F_α.

The primitive species of $T_{sn_1...n_r}$ that have been predicated null do not correspond to anything in M, as they correspond to inhibited sequences, to which the correlation law does not apply. Brouwer (later) called elements that are inhibited while their immediate ascendant is not, 'stops'. The rationale for including the stops in the construction of T is that it guarantees that the generating operation of the second kind employed will indeed have a well-ordered species to add for every ν.

Taken together, the full and null primitive species of $T_{sn_1...n_r}$ correspond to the species τ of secured elements, except that τ also includes extensions of inhibited sequences.

The well-ordering of the thin bar can be further described as follows. Consider any two elements of the thin bar $a = \langle a_0,...,a_m \rangle$ and $b = \langle b_0,...,b_n \rangle$. Because the bar is thin, neither element is a descendant of the other; so even when $m \neq n$, one can indicate the position at which they first differ, say $a_i \neq b_i$. Then T is constructed such that, if $a_i < b_i$ then $a \prec b$, and, conversely, if $b_i < a_i$ then $b \prec a$. So $\langle 2,3,4 \rangle$ comes after $\langle 2,1 \rangle$, and before $\langle 5 \rangle$ (assuming that these sequences are all in a given thin bar). Thus, T is a lexicographical ordering.

4.3 Some comments on Brouwer's proof

1. Each of the well-orderings $T_{sn_1...n_r}$ is constructed strictly upwards; hence, to arrive at them, one never first needs a well-ordering corresponding to a node above $F_{sn_1...n_r}$. As a node's having the well-ordering property implies that it is securable, this suggests that it cannot be essential first to have a canonical proof of the securability of a node higher up in the tree. But this is exactly the direction of argument in a ζ-inference; so ζ-inferences seem redundant. If one proves this independently, this fact can be exploited to prove the bar theorem in a slightly different way. This was done by Brouwer in the 1924 version, which proceeds, in effect, by removing all the ζ-inferences from the canonical proofs (this is done explicitly in an elucidatory companion paper of the same year [18], unfortunately not included in [104], and in the 1954 proof (but see remark 3 below)). The inductive definition of the elements in the thin bar then is a copy of the inductive definition of the resulting canonical proof.

2. While eliminating the ζ-inferences simplifies the proof, the 1927 proof shows that it is not essential to do so, and it is therefore not this eliminability that is the main idea behind the bar theorem. Indeed, in the course of a canonical proof, the securability of a certain $F_{sn_1...n_r}$ may be established more than once, and if it is, there are equally many different proofs of the well-ordering property of that element; but it doesn't matter if there are redundant inferences, in two senses.

It doesn't matter in the sense that in our effort to construct a well-ordering $T_{sn_1...n_r}$, for each ν we need only one well-ordering $T_{sn_1...n_r\nu}$; whether this is obtained from the first proof of the securability of $F_{sn_1...n_r\nu}$, or from a later one, is immaterial. Any one will do.

But as Brouwer mentions in footnote 9 of the 1927 paper, it also doesn't matter in the stronger sense that the well-orderings obtained on the basis of different canonical proofs in fact all come out the same; his term is that they are all 'generation-equivalent'. This is defined as follows [22, pp.452–453]:

- Two well-ordered primitive species F' and F'' are generation-equivalent if they consist of the same element and moreover this element is either full for both or null for both.

- Two well-ordered non-primitive species F' and F'' are generation-equivalent if for arbitrary ν the constructional underspecies F'_ν and F''_ν either both fail to exist, or both exist and are generation-equivalent. [translation taken from [67, p.461]]

(Note that because our species T is generated in the second generating operation, the constructional underspecies T_ν exists for every ν.) What it means for two well-orderings to be generation-equivalent is that although they are different intensionally, as they are defined on the basis of different canonical proofs, they are all built up in exactly the same way. If you would draw them on paper, their pictures would look the same. This is shown by the following induction hinted at by Brouwer.

induction basis

Let $T^k_{sn_1...n_r}$ be a primitive species, corresponding to the canonical proof $k_{sn_1...n_r}$ of the securability of $F_{sn_1...n_r}$.

Assume that there is a different canonical proof of the securability of $F_{sn_1...n_r}$, $m_{sn_1...n_r}$, and let $T^m_{sn_1...n_r}$ be the primitive species corresponding to that.

Now the two species $T^k_{sn_1...n_r}$ and $T^m_{sn_1...n_r}$ are generation-equivalent, because in both cases, the element $F_{sn_1...n_r}$ is the same, and only that determines whether the unique element of $T^k_{sn_1...n_r}$ and $T^m_{sn_1...n_r}$ will be a full or a null element.

induction step

Let $T^k_{sn_1...n_r}$ be a species, built up by adding, in the second generating operation, the species $T^k_{sn_1...n_r\nu}$. The species $T^k_{sn_1...n_r}$ corresponds to the canonical proof $k_{sn_1...n_r}$ of the securability of $F_{sn_1...n_r}$.

Assume that there is a different canonical proof of that, $m_{sn_1...n_r}$, yielding the species $T^m_{sn_1...n_r}$. This species is built up by adding, in the second generating operation, the species $T^m_{sn_1...n_r\nu}$.

By induction hypothesis, for every ν, $T^k_{sn_1...n_r\nu}$ and $T^m_{sn_1...n_r\nu}$ are generation-equivalent: they correspond to different canonical proofs of the securability of the same element $F_{sn_1...n_r\nu}$.

But then, by the definition of generation-equivalence, $T^k_{sn_1...n_r}$ and $T^m_{sn_1...n_r}$ are generation-equivalent.

3. That the bar has to be decidable for the bar theorem to be true was brought to light by Kleene [95, pp.87–88]. Van Dalen gives the following simplified version [37, p.102]. Consider the universal spread and a decidable predicate $A(x)$ for which as yet we have neither a proof of $\forall x A(x)$ nor of $\neg \forall x A(x)$. Now define the species B as follows:

$$\langle \rangle \in B \Leftrightarrow \neg \forall x A(x)$$
$$\langle n \rangle \in B \Leftrightarrow A(n)$$

It will be immaterial what other elements B might contain. Every path α through $\langle \rangle$ hits B, so B is a bar. This is seen as follows. For any particular $\alpha(0)$—the first value on the path α—we can always find out whether A holds of it or not, for it was given that $A(x)$ is decidable. If it holds, then $\langle \alpha(0) \rangle \in B$; if it doesn't, then we have a counterexample to $\forall x A(x)$, therefore $\neg \forall x A(x)$, and $\langle \rangle \in B$.

B is, at present, not a decidable bar. For if it were, then, in particular, $\langle \rangle \in B \vee \langle \rangle \notin B$. Combining this with the intuitionistically valid $\neg\neg \forall x A(x) \to \forall x \neg\neg A(x)$ and with $\forall x \neg\neg A(x) \to \forall x A(x)$, valid because A is decidable, we obtain $\neg \forall x A(x) \vee \forall x A(x)$; but this contradicts our hypothesis that we do not yet have a proof of the latter.

Now assume that the bar theorem holds for this B, so that it contains a well-ordered thin bar B'; being a well-ordered species, B' is decidable. It follows that, in particular, $\langle \rangle \in B' \vee \langle \rangle \notin B'$. But then we get, by the same reasoning as above, $\neg \forall x A(x) \vee \forall x A(x)$, contradiction. Thus, we have a weak counterexample to the bar theorem for bars that are not decidable: it is not shown that it is false, but it is shown that it cannot be true as long as there are such predicates A satifying the conditions mentioned.

I mentioned that the decidability of the bar is implicit in the premises of the 1924 and 1927 proofs of the bar theorem (because of the continuity principle), but it is neither explicit nor implicit in the proof from 1954. The countexample shows, therefore, that the latter proof must be incorrect. For further discussion, see [107] and [49, 3.4].

4. Various authors—Heyting, Kleene, Troelstra, Dummett—agree with Brouwer's remark on securability in his footnote 7, quoted on p.50 above. They choose to adopt that in the form of the axiom schema BI_D for bars in the universal spread (one axiom for each specific bar). It has the form of an implication, where the antecedent consists of a conjunction of four conditions. For

clarity, I will write each conjunct on a new line:

$$BI_D \qquad \forall \alpha \exists x (\bar{\alpha}x \in B) \land \qquad (4.1)$$
$$\forall n(n \in B \lor n \notin B) \land \qquad (4.2)$$
$$\forall n(n \in B \to n \in Q) \land \qquad (4.3)$$
$$\forall n(\forall y(n*y \in Q) \to n \in Q) \to \qquad (4.4)$$
$$\langle\rangle \in Q \qquad (4.5)$$

(4.1) expresses that B is a bar (not necessarily thin). (4.2) adds to this that B is decidable—hence the 'D' in BI_D. Let Q be the species of securable sequences; then (4.3) specfies that whenever an element is in the bar, it is securable. In (4.4), $n*y$ means the element n extended by one choice y. For example, $\langle 1, 2, 3\rangle *$ 4 is $\langle 1, 2, 3, 4\rangle$. (4.4) translates Brouwer's stipulation that securability is the property that, whenever it holds for all immediate descendants of an element, holds for that element itself. The conclusion drawn from (4.1)–(4.4) is that the root of the tree is securable (4.5).

As explained after the quote from Brouwer's footnote on p.51, BI_D immediately implies the well-ordering property for any $F_{sn_1...n_r}$ in σ, and in particular for the root $\langle\rangle$; so if one finds BI_D evident, one can leave aside the long argument based on analysis of proofs into canonical proofs. Of particular interest is Kleene's proof that BI_D is independent of the other intuitionistic principles as he formalized them [95, p.113]. This means that if one wishes to prove the validity of the schema, one has to adopt a new principle in its place to prove it from; and Kleene remarks, 'We are unconvinced that any known substitute is more fundamental and intuitive' [95, p.51]. But as we have seen, the substitute of the analysis in terms of canonical proofs is more fundamental in the sense that it makes the role of intentionality in proofs explicit. Perhaps one should consider the long proof first of all an explication of the principle in the footnote [75, p.45]. Indeed, it has been shown by Martino and Giaretta that Brouwer's claim that any proof of the existence of a bar can be analysed into his three elementary inferences is, if one accepts the continuity principle, equivalent to BI_D [107].[33] Brouwer sometimes wondered if the basic relations on which the elementary inferences are based couldn't be reduced to even more basic relations [34, p.13]. This is still an open question (see p.65).

4.4 The fan theorem

From the bar theorem, Brouwer proved the fan theorem. In turn, the fan theorem is used to prove that all total functions on the continuum (intuitionistically conceived) are continuous, and uniformly continuous at that. The importance of this result was explained at the beginning of this chapter.

Recall that a spread M is a finitary tree or fan if each node in it has only finitely many immediate descendants. (According to the definition of a spread, it always has at least one.) Intuitionistically, 'each node has only finitely many descendants' means 'for each node (in the underlying tree) we can determine a number k such that no choice greater than k is admissible at that node'. If we cannot do this, then we don't know that M is a fan. Brouwer states the fan theorem as follows:

> If with each element e of a finitary spread M a natural number β_e is associated, a natural number z can be specified such that β_e is completely determined by the first z choices generating e. [21, p.462]

The point is that, while β_e in general will depend on finite elements in the underlying tree and the correlation law, it does not depend on any infinite choice sequence.

One can prove that the unit continuum, i.e. the closed interval $[0,1]$, can be represented by a fan, for example the fan J we saw earlier, p.43.[34] (To do this, one has to show that every element of the fan falls within that interval and that, conversely, every element of that interval coincides with an element of the fan. An open interval cannot be represented by a fan as in such an interval there is no leftmost element and no rightmost element.) From this, Brouwer proved the uniform continuity theorem: a total function from the closed interval $[0,1]$ to $\mathbb{R}$ is uniformly continuous on $[0,1]$, that is, in a standard formulation,

$$\forall \epsilon \exists \delta \forall x_1 \forall x_2 (|x_1 - x_2| < \delta \rightarrow |f(x_1) - f(x_2)| < \epsilon)$$

for positive δ, ϵ and $x_1, x_2 \in [0,1]$.

An immediate consequence (a matter of manipulating the quantifiers in front) of the uniform continuity theorem is the continuity theorem, which is not stated by Brouwer: a total function from the closed interval $[0,1]$ to $\mathbb{R}$ is continuous on $[0,1]$, that is, again in a standard formulation,

$$\forall \epsilon \forall x_1 \exists \delta \forall x_2 (|x_1 - x_2| < \delta \rightarrow |f(x_1) - f(x_2)| < \epsilon)$$

for positive δ, ϵ and $x_1, x_2 \in [0,1]$.

One can see from the order of the quantifiers why the uniform continuity theorem is a stronger result than the continuity theorem: for a given ϵ, uniform continuity demands that the same δ work for all x_1 simultaneously, whereas for ordinary continuity, δ may vary with each x_1. It is therefore plausible that uniform continuity should require knowledge of the structure of the bar whereas ordinary continuity does not.[35] The uniform continuity theorem is a much more powerful weapon than the continuity theorem; this will have added to Brouwer's pride in having established it.

An important consequence of the continuity theorem[36] is the unsplittability of the unit continuum: suppose $[0,1] = A \cup B$ and $A \cap B = \emptyset$, then f defined by

$$f(x) = \begin{cases} 0 & \text{if } x \in A \\ 1 & \text{if } x \in B \end{cases}$$

is total and therefore, by the continuity theorem, continuous. But then f must be constant, so either $[0,1] = A$ or $[0,1] = B$.

These results for the unit continuum—continuity, uniform continuity, and unsplittability—generalize to the whole continuum. A remarkable consequence is that it is false that every real number is either rational or irrational. For if it were, we could obtain a splitting of the continuum by assigning 0 to rational, and 1 to irrational real numbers.[37] This is a strong counterexample to one form of the principle of excluded middle:

$$\neg \forall x \in \mathbb{R}(x \in \mathbb{Q} \vee x \notin \mathbb{Q})$$

Note that this does not mean that it is contradictory to hold of any particular real number c that it is rational or irrational; but it does mean that it is contradictory to hold it for all real numbers simultaneously.

The fan theorem, from which Brouwer derived these results, holds for the special kind of spread that fans are, but not for spreads in general. Here is a counterexample. Consider the universal spread and define a function f on it by $f(\alpha) = \alpha(\alpha(0))$, that is, f assigns to α the value of its $\alpha(0)$-th element. As α is an element of the universal spread, this means that any arbitrary choice for $\alpha(0)$ is admitted. But then there can be no upper bound on $\alpha(0)$, and hence not on the length of the segment of any α that one has to know before one can determine $f(\alpha)$. In this case there is no z as claimed by the fan theorem.

Before looking at how the fan theorem follows from the bar theorem, let us first, as we did above for the bar theorem, see why a certain simple-minded approach doesn't work (compare [52], the general tenet of which however I do not accept). Start at the root of the underlying tree and try all admissible paths of length 1. This can be done as in a fan we know that there are only finitely many. Put all paths that just hit the bar aside; of the remaining ones, now try their admissible immediate extensions. In other words, try all admissible paths of length 2 such that their predecessor hasn't hit the bar already. Of these there are likewise only finitely many. Put all paths that just hit the bar aside, etc. Keep repeating the process; as every infinite path will at some point hit the bar, the process will end. The length at which all paths of that length are put aside is the maximum length a path can have in this fan when it hits the bar. This is the z we were looking for.

However, this reasoning is circular. To know that the process will end means, intuitionistically, that we can determine an upper bound on the length of paths to the thin bar. But that we can is precisely what we are trying to prove.

This is where the bar theorem comes in. As the fan is barred by a decidable bar, the bar theorem applies, and yields a well-ordered thin bar. That well-ordering is constructed using generating operations of the second kind. This operation adds together infinitely many well-ordered species $T_{sn_1...n_r\nu}$ that are determined by the rules we saw on p.55. In particular, $T_{sn_1...n_r\nu}$ will be a null element exactly if choosing ν does not yield an admissible extension of $F_{sn_1...n_r}$.

Now, given that M is a fan, we know that there are always only finitely many admissible extensions. That is, for each $F_{sn_1...n_r}$ we can indicate a number k such that for all $\nu > k$, $F_{sn_1...n_r\nu}$ is inadmissible. But then for all $\nu > k$, $T_{sn_1...n_r\nu}$ will be a null element. If we go through the $T_{sn_1...n_r\nu}$, starting at

61

$T_{sn_1...n_r0}$, then all the elements among them that are not null will have been reached, at the latest, by the time we have arrived at $T_{sn_1...n_rk}$. Let these elements form the content of a species $Q_{sn_1...n_r}$. It can be constructed as a well-ordered species in parallel with $T_{sn_1...n_r}$, this time using a generating operation of the first kind. When $T_{sn_1...n_r0}$ to $T_{sn_1...n_rk}$ have been determined, run through them to determine the summands whose sum will be $Q_{sn_1...n_r}$, as follows:

- If $T_{sn_1...n_r\nu}$ is a primitive species consisting of ν as a null element, and therefore corresponds to an inadmissible element and determines no element of M, we skip it.

- If $T_{sn_1...n_r\nu}$ is a primitive species consisting of ν as a full element, we put a primitive species $Q_{sn_1...n_r\nu}$ consisting of ν as a full element next in the list of summands.

- In the remaining case, where $T_{sn_1...n_r\nu}$ is not a primitive species, we appeal to our backward induction hypothesis, by which we already have a well-ordered species $Q_{sn_1...n_r\nu}$; we put this species next in the list of summands.

Adding the summands on the finite list in a generating operation of the first kind, we obtain $Q_{sn_1...n_r}$. It has only full elements and no null ones. We constructed it using only generating operations of the first kind, so the species of its elements must be finite, as is shown by an easy induction. Because of the way it is constructed, $Q_{sn_1...n_r}$ determines a well-ordering of the species of full elements of $T_{sn_1...n_r}$, which therefore is also finite.

In particular, the species of full elements of $T_{()}$—the species, that is, of all nodes in the thin bar μ_1—is well-ordered and finite. In that case, a natural number z can be indicated such that the maximum length of a path from the root to the bar is z: just run through the finite well-ordering of full elements of $T_{()}$ and keep track of the deepest node found so far. As it takes at most z choices to hit the bar from the root, the natural number β_e assigned to an element e of M is completely determined by the first z choices generating e. This proves the fan theorem.

From a classical point of view, one proves the same much quicker, from König's lemma:[38]

> If a fan contains infinitely many nodes, it contains an infinite path

Taking the contraposition gives

> If a fan contains only finite paths, it contains finitely many nodes (and hence there is an upper bound on the length of the paths)

Note that a spread that has only finite paths can still contain infinitely many nodes: not in depth, but in width. But such a spread is not a fan. As a bar in a fan cuts off all infinite paths at some point, it determines a fan having only finite paths, and if we then apply the contraposition of König's lemma to that, we obtain a classical version of the fan theorem.

But this version does not have the same strong content as the intuitionistic one, for the latter provides us with a construction of an upper bound. The classical version merely says that there is such a bound, without further informing us what this bound is. This is why the move of contraposing König's lemma is not intuitionistically valid: it introduces an existential statement without supplying a construction to find a number that is a witness to it. But then we have, on the intuitionistic interpretation of logic, no right to hold that statement true.

It might be instructive to see why the classical proof of König's lemma itself is not intuitionistically valid; the reason why also shows that there is little reason to suppose that König's lemma is intuitionistically true at all.

The proof has a certain constructive flavour, as it defines an infinite path α through the fan inductively [134, p.8]. We let the path start at the root, which has, by hypothesis, infinitely many descendants, and set $\alpha(0) = \langle \rangle$. This is the induction basis. The induction step is based on the observation that, of the finite number of immediate descendants that a node $\alpha(n)$ in the fan has, at least one must have infinitely many descendants. For if none had, then the fan couldn't contain infinitely many nodes, as it does, by the hypothesis of the theorem. Pick such an immediate descendant for $\alpha(n+1)$, the next node on the infinite path α. By induction from the root down, then, we have defined $\alpha(n)$ for all values of n, and this determines an infinite path, as was asked for.

This proof, however, is not really constructive. It employs the principle of the excluded middle in the form 'Each immediate descendant either has finitely many descendants, or it has infinitely many'. But it is not effectively decidable which is the case, and therefore it is not intuitionistically true. Obviously, a trial-and-error search for an immediate descendant of $\alpha(n)$ that has infinitely many descendants is out of the question; and neither do we have another general method to determine one. In a specific fan of course the spread law may be such that from inspecting it we can, at any given node, effectively pick out such an immediate descendant as required; but there is no reason to suppose that this is the case for every fan.

König's lemma was proved in 1926, two years after Brouwer's first proof of the fan theorem. Historically, the two results seem to be unrelated. It is of some interest that here we have a theorem of which the intuitionistic proof preceded the classical one.

Chapter 5

'Creating Subject' arguments

As Brouwer defines mathematics by the free activity of the creating subject, one could maintain that every argument in intuitionistic mathematics should be called a 'creating subject argument'. Although in itself this would be an entirely appropriate suggestion, the term has traditionally been reserved for the particular type of argument that depends on the following feature of the creating subject: if, of a given proposition p, the creating subject comes to know that it will never prove it, that is a sufficient ground for the subject to conclude that p is false. If we write 'the subject has experienced p at time n' as $\square_n p$, the feature can be put into the following formula:

$$\neg \exists n \square_n p \to \neg p \qquad \text{(PIN)}$$

(PIN for 'from perpetual ignorance to negation'.)

From the classical point of view, on which it is perfectly conceivable that a proposition that will never be proved is nevertheless true, PIN is surprising; and so it is from the perspective of other varieties of constructive mathematics, where it is perfectly conceivable that a proposition has a proof but that for some reason it will never be found.

Accepting PIN is far from inconsequential; Brouwer used it to furnish counterexamples, weak and strong, to classically valid statements. For example, in 1948 [30] he showed

$$\neg \forall x \in \mathbb{R}(\neg \neg x > 0 \to x > 0)$$

That is, he showed the following. If you assume that for every real number its being not not positive amounts to its being positive, you are assuming something that is false. Note that Brouwer is not playing here the familiar intuitionistic tune that we have no reason, in general, to assume that for all x, from $\neg \neg P(x)$, $P(x)$ follows; he is modulating to saying that there are cases where it is actually contradictory to make that assumption. (In interpreting this particular case, one has to keep in mind that, as explained in chapter 3, the intuitionistic $\mathbb{R}$ is different from its classical counterpart.)

Yet the philosophical interest of PIN cannot be the mere fact that it leads to counterexamples; for these can already be obtained without it, also strong ones. An example we saw in the chapter on the bar theorem:

$$\neg \forall x \in \mathbb{R}(x \in \mathbb{Q} \vee x \notin \mathbb{Q})$$

which followed from the continuity theorem. Rather, what is of philosophical interest is the way PIN is motivated. It makes apparent properties of the creating subject that so far did not stand out.

To see this motivation, let us first go back to the proof of the bar theorem in the previous chapter. It depends on properties of the creating subject in the following two ways: truth of a proposition consists in its having been experienced (or proved) by the subject, and such experiences (proofs) have an inner structure. Thus, the subject's knowledge that a certain species B is a bar consists in its having a proof that B is a bar, which was then explicated: what is the inner structure of a proof of a bar? This turned out to be an intentional structure that admitted of a well-ordering; the explication was the key to establishing the bar theorem.

The study of a mathematical experience in the proof of the bar theorem was first of all guided, in a term of Husserl's not used by Brouwer, by the inner horizon of that experience. This concept can be explained as follows. In the experience, at any instant, of any object, not all properties of that object are actually given to us. But an object is always an object of a certain type, so there are always a number of determinations typical for that kind of object that we can expect to make. For example, if we know that something is a proof then we know that as such it is made up from steps, and we can then turn to determining the steps, finding steps to fill gaps, or analysing given steps into more elementary ones. The inner horizon is what separates the actually given properties from possible further determinations of the experienced object; in our example, from further determinations of the proof that B is a bar. In his proof of the bar theorem Brouwer stops exploring the inner horizon when he has reached the three elementary proof steps, as they suffice for his purposes. When he explicitly raises the question whether these elementary steps admit of an even deeper analysis, he is in effect acknowledging that finding these steps at the same time pushed back the inner horizon.

Husserl noticed that experiences of objects have, besides an inner horizon, an outer horizon that points to other objects. It is the outer horizon that makes these various objects cohere, in however minimal a way. An object that wouldn't be referred to in the outer horizon of the experience of any other object would be completely isolated, approachable from nowhere, hence inaccessible to experience.

If we try to apply the concept of the outer horizon to mathematics, the question becomes how individual mathematical experiences are related to one another. At first it might seem that the answer lies in the consequence relation.

But that relation presupposes a more fundamental one, because before the subject can judge whether one experienced truth is a consequence of another, there has to be something to which they both belong and out of which they can be selected. If mathematical experiences wouldn't each have a place in a structure that thereby relates them to one another, there couldn't be a systematic study of them; there could be no mathematics. What, then, is the structure that makes the creating subject's activities cohere?

The basic insight is that the various mathematical activities of the subject are all carried out in discrete stages in a single flow of time. From Brouwer's work it is clear that, reflecting on this insight, he discerned several properties of the structure this imposes. Instead of formulating these explicitly he used them in his arguments; an example of such an argument we will see below. The formulation of the axioms left implicit by Brouwer is due to Kreisel [99] and Kripke:

$$p \leftrightarrow \exists n \Box_n p \qquad \text{(Sub1)}$$

In words: p is true exactly if the creating subject has full evidence for it at some moment.

$$\forall n \forall m (\Box_n p \to \Box_{n+m} p) \qquad \text{(Sub2)}$$

Experiences are never forgotten.

$$\forall n (\Box_n p \vee \neg \Box_n p) \qquad \text{(Sub3)}$$

At every moment the creating subject can decide whether it has experienced p or not.

A reminder of the exact role of language in intuitionistic mathematics may be in place here. As Stanley Rosen has aptly remarked,

> Analytical philosophy ... objectifies the subject, or overlooks the presence of the subject in the structure of the proposition ... This tendency is illustrated in the attempt by Kreisel and others to mathematize Brouwer's conception of the creative subject as expressing the force of mathematics, a force that cannot itself be expressed in mathematical terms. [121, p.186]

And indeed, an objectified subject can by no stretch of the imagination replace the creating subject; yet, we can fix some of our insights into the nature of the creating subject in axioms that facilitate our reasoning about it.

The biconditional Sub1 can be analysed into its two components:

$$p \to \exists n \Box_n p \qquad \text{(Sub1a)}$$
$$\exists n \Box_n p \to p \qquad \text{(Sub1b)}$$

Intuitionistically, Sub1a is justified as follows. If p is true, this means it has been experienced; but if it has been, then the subject can construct a number m that corresponds to the moment in time at which that experience occurred. It is, after all, essential to an experience that it occurs at a certain moment in time. In particular, there is no mathematics outside time.

The correctness of (Sub1b) is seen from the fact that for the creating subject, to experience p at some point is a sufficient condition for the truth of p.

Let us see why it follows from Sub1 that, as PIN expresses, if the creating subject knows that p will never be proved, then p is false.

Assume
$$\neg \exists n \Box_n p \tag{1}$$
that is,
$$\exists n \Box_n p \to \bot \tag{2}$$
Combining (Sub1a) and (2), we get
$$p \to \bot \tag{3}$$
For if we would have a proof of p, then we would have obtained it at a certain moment m, so $\Box_m p$, and we could then introduce an existential quantifier and obtain the antecedent of (2). An application of modus ponens gives (3), which, by definition, is equivalent to
$$\neg p \tag{4}$$
This shows for (Sub1a) specifically what is true in general, namely, that the contraposition of a true implication is again intuitionistically true. In this case, the contraposition turned out to be PIN; within the intuitionistic framework, then, PIN is not surprising at all.

That in other philosophies of mathematics PIN is not true has its ground in their different answer to the question what the conditions of 'p is true' are. As we saw in chapter 1, Brouwer's reply is that the one condition for the truth of p is that p has been experienced, and this is used in the argument, in the form of (Sub1a), to pass from (2) to (3). In chapter 2, I discussed reasons why a tenseless notion of truth ('p is true if it can be experienced/proved' or 'if it is experiencable/provable') is unacceptable to Brouwer. However, if one does accept such a notion, (Sub1a) fails, and there is no longer reason to hold that (4) follows from (1), as (3) can no longer be inferred from (2). From the actual, tenseless existence of a proof we cannot conclude that at some time we will actually know that proof without invoking a principle of plenitude—a principle to the effect that everything that can be proved, will be proved.

There is also a weaker form of Sub1,
$$(p \to \neg\neg \exists n \Box_n p) \land (\exists n \Box_n p \to p)$$
The second conjunct is the same as Sub1b, but here the first conjunct expresses that if p is true, then it is impossible that the creating subject will never prove it (the creating subject is free to prove whatever it can); on the intuitionistic reading of logic, that is to say less than that the subject will prove it at some point. In the literature, Sub1 as well this weaker form go by the name of 'Principle of Christian Charity', or, alternatively, the 'Principle of Infinite Vanity' (both coined by Kreisel). Given the justication of Sub1 from the intuitionistic conception of truth, it is clear that for their delightfully dramatic ring these names rely on remnants of platonism, see [49, p.242].

Let us now consider a weak counterexample that for its construction depends on PIN, adapted from Brouwer [30]. It will, for a different reason, also figure in the chapter 6 on intersubjectivity. The counterexample in question has to do with the notion of apartness of two real numbers: $a \# b \equiv \exists n(|a - b| > 2^{-n})$. This is stronger than $\neg(a = b)$, for to know that a and b are apart from one another, you not only have to know that they cannot be equal, but also need some positive information on how large the difference is. Correspondingly, the weak counterexample consists in showing that we have no reason to assume

$$\forall x \in \mathbb{R}(x \neq 0 \to x \# 0)$$

The argument takes its cue, as usual, from an assertion p for which we have as yet proved neither p nor $\neg p$, for example, as usual, Goldbach's conjecture (see p.26). Now the creating subject defines a real number α in a choice sequence of rational numbers $\alpha_1, \alpha_2, \alpha_3, \ldots$, as follows:

- As long as, during the choice of the α_n, neither p nor $\neg p$ has been experienced by the creating subject, each α_n is chosen to be 0.

- As soon as between the choice of α_{r-1} and α_r, p has been experienced by the creating subject, α_r and all further choices will be fixed to $(\frac{1}{2})^r$.

- Should, on the contrary, between the choice of α_{s-1} and α_s, $\neg p$ have has been experienced by the creating subject, α_s and all further choices will be fixed to $-(\frac{1}{2})^s$.

This choice sequence $\alpha_1, \alpha_2, \alpha_3, \ldots$ converges, as for every n, the choices made after the n-th, however they turn out, lie within $(\frac{1}{2})^n$ of each other. So as n increases, this possible difference becomes smaller. Thus, the choice sequence determines a real number α; note that α is a lawlike choice sequence.

Now, $\alpha = 0 \Leftrightarrow \neg(p \lor \neg p)$, for the subject can only know that all choices will come out 0 if it knows that neither p nor $\neg p$ will ever be proved, which, because of PIN, would mean that $p \lor \neg p$ is false. Of course, that is not possible, so the subject knows that in fact $\neg\neg(p \lor \neg p)$, and therefore knows that $\alpha \neq 0$.

For the real number α, it is also true, by definition, that $\alpha \# 0 \Leftrightarrow \exists n \alpha_n \neq 0$, so it cannot be proved by the subject that $\alpha \# 0$ until it has a proof of $p \lor \neg p$, that is, until it has proved or disproved p. By hypothesis, it hasn't done so yet; thus, this is a weak counterexample to $\forall x(x \neq 0 \leftrightarrow x \# 0)$.

In 1949 Brouwer devised a technique, involving PIN and the fan theorem discussed in the previous chapter, by which this weak counterexample can be strengthened to a strong one [31]:

$$\neg \forall x \in \mathbb{R}(x \neq 0 \to x \# 0)$$

(A perspicuous proof is presented by Heyting [75, pp.121–122]). As we had occasion to note in a similar case (in the discussion of fan theorem), this strong counterexample does not mean that of any specific real number c it is contradictory to hold $c \neq 0 \to c \# 0$; it means that it is contradictory to suppose this of all real numbers at once.

It is remarkable that the structure of the creating subject's activity turns out to be the same as that of a choice sequence: a potentially infinite, open-ended series of discrete stages. It is clear that Brouwer recognized this structural identity. Not only did he use, in the construction of counterexamples such as the one we just saw, choice sequences to record mathematical activity, but, as we saw in chapter 1, he came to say that the second act of intuitionism (in which choice sequences are recognized as mathematical objects) is an immediate consequence of the first (in which mathematical activity is defined by the self-unfolding of the intuition of two-ity).

This structural identity can be made explicit as a mathematical principle, as follows. The creating subject can associate with each proposition p a choice sequence α that functions as a log in which the subject registers its progress, or lack thereof, in its dealings with p:

$$\alpha(n) = \begin{cases} 0 & \text{if } \neg\square_n p, \\ 1 & \text{else} \end{cases}$$

So the values in α will be 0 as long as the subject has not obtained a proof of p, and 1 afterward. Now 'Kripke's Schema' (a term introduced by Myhill [113]) is the axiom schema which allows one to derive, for any particular p, that such an associated α exists:

$$\exists \alpha (p \leftrightarrow \exists x (\alpha(x) = 1)) \tag{KS}$$

Brouwer stated KS in 1954 [34, first sentence of penultimate paragraph on p.4] as was pointed out by Myhill in 1967 [113]; but Brouwer never used it. KS is of interest for various reasons:

1. it shows an application of choice sequences outside analysis;

2. it illustrates how the creating subject can make use of typically intuitionistic objects in reasoning about its own activity;

3. it suffices to construct the counterexamples, it contains what is needed from Sub1–3 and can be derived from them. It is therefore often found in the literature.

A further reason could have been that KS doesn't mention the creating subject and the time parameter explicitly; some people feel uncomfortable with them. But intuitionistically, Kripke's schema is justified in these very terms.

Sub1 (and the implied PIN) have been said to embody the 'solipsistic aspect' of the creating subject: if a proposition is true, then the subject knows it at some stage. I already mentioned that, on the intuitionistic construal of truth, this was only to be expected. In the chapter 6, I will argue that this 'solipsism' does not preclude intersubjective agreement; so perhaps 'self-sufficient' would fit the creating subject even better than 'solipsistic'.

Kreisel once gave a non-solipsistic axiomatization, or one in which this self-sufficiency is not made explicit. There, p is set equivalent to 'there is a subject that has at some stage obtained evidence for p'. The result is weaker than KS

[134, p.241]. This is as one would expect; in particular none of the various subjects now can, if it knows that it will not prove p, conclude $\neg p$ anymore: perhaps one of the other subjects will prove p. Of course such a reading was not acceptable to Brouwer, who said that 'expected experiences and experiences attributed to others are only true as anticipations and hypotheses; in their content there is no truth' [29, p.1243].

Van Dalen has proved a converse of Brouwer's unsplittability theorem: KS and $\mathbb{R}$ is unsplittable $\Rightarrow$ there are no discontinuous real functions [44, p.252]. This shows how powerful the mathematical consequences of the notion of the creating subject can be.

A refinement of our analysis so far should be mentioned that exposes yet another aspect of the structure of the creating subject's activity. It is due to the Dutch intuitionist Troelstra [132].

The creating subject establishes at each stage of its activity one new result, in addition to keeping in mind all the previous ones (Sub2). The subject can keep a list of those new results, $P(0), P(1), P(2), \ldots$ For example, $P(6)$ could be $2 + 2 = 4$, $P(199)$ 'the next choice in lawless sequence γ is 3', $P(25536)$ 'π is irrational', and so on; in particular, some of them will consist in the judgment (or decision) that a certain choice sequence α is fixed by a recipe (possibly referring to the subject's activity, thus going beyond the strictly lawlike). Let us write such a result as $R(\alpha)$. Now the subject can define a sequence β by

$$\beta(n) = \begin{cases} \alpha(n) + 1 & \text{if } P(n) \text{ is } R(\alpha) \text{ for some } \alpha \\ 0 & \text{if } P(n) \text{ is of a different kind} \end{cases}$$

In effect, the sequence β is a bookkeeping device that records the times at which the subject judged that a given choice sequence is fixed by a recipe. The sequence β is itself fixed by a recipe [134, p.845]. But this leads to a paradox. If $R(\beta)$ is true, then by Sub1a,

$$\exists n \Box_n R(\beta)$$

Let us say that $R(\beta)$ is established at time k:

$$\Box_k R(\beta)$$

Then $P(k)$ is $R(\beta)$, hence, by definition of β,

$$\beta(k) = \beta(k) + 1$$

which is a contradiction.

The problem is caused by the impredicativity of the definition of β: the sequence is defined in terms of all of the subject's activities, but creating this sequence is itself one of them.

I will adopt Troelstra's term 'self-reflection' for activities that involve reference to the course of the subject's other activities. Self-reflection is, in itself, not problematic. We saw a harmless self-reflection in the weak counterexample to $\forall x(x \neq 0 \to x\#0)$ above. In other cases, such as β, however, it is, as we just saw, illicit. The subject can rule out such cases by imposing a hierarchy on its activities (assertions and constructions), thus applying Russell's vicious circle principle: 'Whatever involves all of a collection must not be one of the collection'. The levels in the hierarchy are defined by induction:

level 0: activities involving no self-reflection, e.g. $1 + 1 = 2$
level n: activities involving only reflection on activities of at most level $n - 1$

Activities are then considered legitimate only if they have a place in this hierarchy. For example, as activities at level 1 will either be of level 0 or involve reflection but only on activities at level 0, the weak counterexample above operates at level 1. It involves reflection on whether or not the subject has proved a proposition p, in this case Goldbach's conjecture, which does not explicitly refer to any of the subject's activity. It is assumed that, if an assertion at level n has a proof, it has one of level n. A precise specification of a construction involving reflection now demands that the levels of the activities to which reference is made, be specified; the reflection itself will, by definition of the hierarchy, be of a level at least one higher than the highest among them. But then the reflection cannot itself occur among the activities reflected on, and this blocks the argument that led to the paradox. Specifically, one has to fix a level of the activities to which the definition of β refers, and then β itself will occur no sooner than at the first level above all of them; moreover, the judgment 'β is lawlike' is again one level higher, so it is excluded that it plays a role in β.

We spoke of the subject's imposing a hierarchy on its activities, but perhaps it is more appropriate to speak of its recognizing a hierarchy: for, as Dummett [49, p.241] notices, it is hardly plausible that the creating subject could have been understanding a genuinely impredicative notion such as the unrestricted $\square_n$, only to drop it when the paradox appeared. The domain of applicability of the unrestricted notion cannot be indicated independently of that notion itself; but then it is unclear how the subject ever could arrive at a full understanding of it. It was the same reason, of course, that led Brouwer to stipulate that a species is a property 'supposable for mathematical entities previously acquired' [32, p.511], [37, p.8, footnote 2].

Stealing the conclusion of this chapter from Troelstra [132, p.107] makes me a happy thief: 'We might say that the theory of the creative subject is provocative, attractive, and dangerous; it represents the extreme consequences of intuitionistic subjectivism; undoubtedly it deserves further study, precisely for this reason.'

Chapter 6

Intersubjectivity

Brouwer characteristically insists that mathematics is not about an independent reality, but about constructions that the individual makes in its mind. There is a traditional suspicion that this tenet makes intuitionism defenceless against the charges of psychologism, understood as the thesis that mathematical truths are truths of empirical psychology, and of subjectivism, the thesis that the truths of mathematics may vary with each subject.[39] Hilbert, for example, wrote in 1928:

> It is part of the task of science to liberate us from arbitrariness, sentiment, and habit and to protect us from the subjectivism that already made itself felt in Kronecker's views and, it seems to me, finds it culmination in intuitionism. [78, p.475]

Indeed, why should the constructions that different individuals make in their minds lead to the same results? Doesn't this mean that everyone has their own mathematics? Someone who thinks of mathematics as describing an independent realm, as Gödel did, or, as being founded on language, as the later Wittgenstein did, is free of this problem that seems to face the intuitionist. (I once heard the Dutch mathematician N.G. de Bruijn tell the following anecdote. One intuitionist mathematician wondered out loud to another, 'This *mind* in which intuitionistic mathematics takes place, is that my mind?' To which the other replied, 'No, Brouwer's mind!')

As a possible reply to such charges against intuitionism, one occasionally finds the suggestion that the intuitionistic subject, the 'creating subject' to use Brouwer's term, should be thought of as a transcendental subject instead of a psychological one. On such an interpretation, it is possible to find an reply to the charges of psychologism and subjectivism. This suggestion has been made by, for example, Mohanty [111], Placek [116], Posy [117, 118], and Roberts [120].

I want to amplify this suggestion in two ways.

First, I will support it by a piece of historical evidence recently found in the Brouwer Archive.

Second, I will defend a claim that the creating subject is best understood as a transcendental subject in the sense of Husserl. With the exception of Roberts, the authors mentioned all think of the transcendental subject in Kant's sense. Although Roberts does not give arguments why he prefers a Husserlian interpretation over a Kantian one, I will argue that there are good reasons to do so.

6.1 Intuitionism and the threat of psychologism

As we have seen in the preceding chapters, intuitionistic mathematics is a free, but not arbitrary, creation of the mind. The objects in intuitionism exist only in so far as the creating subject has built them.

Compare this characterization with the following words of Frege, from the Grundgesetze der Arithmetik:

> If we could grasp nothing but what is in ourselves, then a [genuine] conflict of opinions, [as well as] a reciprocity of understanding, would be impossible, since there would be no common ground, and no idea in the psychological sense can be such a ground. There would be no logic that can be appealed to as arbiter in the conflict of opinions. [53, p.206, adapted]

And in a letter from 1906 to that other champion of anti-psychologism, Husserl, Frege wrote,

> The logicians ... are too much caught up in psychology ... Logic in no way is a part of psychology. The Pythagorean Theorem expresses the same thought for all men, while each person has its own representations, feelings, and resolutions that are different from those of every other person. Thoughts are not psychic structures, and thinking is not an inner producing and forming, but an apprehension of thoughts which are already objectively given. [110, p.122]

Although neither Frege nor Husserl ever commented on the issue of intuitionism and psychologism, it lies close to hand to do it for them. Indeed, several commentators have offered psychologistic readings of intuitionism, in which the creating subject is identified with a psychological subject. One can find this identification in, for example, Mannoury [105, p.131], Dummett [48, p.609], and Parsons [115, p.213–214]. (It should be noted that among them, Mannoury is the one who values a psychologistic interpretation positively.)

In a psychologistic interpretation of mathematics, the problem of intersubjectivity looms large. Placek, in his monograph on the particular problem of intersubjectivity and intuitionism, considers two alternative conditions for intersubjectivity.

First, the mentalist condition: For two people to communicate, their perceptional contents, thoughts or memories should contain some invariant element, common to all thinking human subjects;

and second, the Wittgensteinian condition: In the process of language-learning, people should be able to acquire abilities to use linguistic expressions in basically the same way. This condition might be meant to address worries that Brouwer's intuitionism falls prey to a private language argument. I think that in the interpretation of the creating subject as Husserl's transcendental subject, it does not. I will come back to this later.

Frege would say that the mentalist condition is fulfilled because different people can grasp the same objective thought. Does Brouwer have a reply to the charge that intuitionism is a psychologism and therefore cannot fulfill the mentalist condition?

6.2 Brouwer's denial of psychologism

That Brouwer did not intend intuitionism to be a psychologism is clear from a remark he makes in a book review in 1911. He says there that psychology cannot be used to justify the axioms, definitions and rules of inference accepted in mathematics, because

> like every science of experience (i.e. generalization of experience) psychology presupposes mathematics at least up to the first infinite cardinal number inclusive. [14, p.121]

While the intention is clear, the argument is not very persuasive. This is because, as Husserl had pointed out some years before [86, p.69], 'presupposes' is ambiguous. It may mean to act according to certain principles, or to have these as explicit premises. Only in the latter case it would be question-begging to found mathematics on psychology. (The first reading is in fact supported by a passage in one of the drafts of Brouwer's dissertation that reads, 'Mathematics is not itself a science, but a moment in the act which doing science is' [46, p.147]. A passage in the 'Signific Dialogues' (held in 1922, published in 1937 [40]) is sometimes taken to show that Brouwer (at least at that time) upheld a psychologistic interpretation of mathematics [64, p.92]. He there calls truth 'a general emotional phenomenon' (p.451), and says that 'the sentiment of mathematical truth' is 'a feeling of complete satisfaction' (p.452). It is not clear whether Brouwer was going through a genuinely psychologistic phase here, or whether, in an effort to contrast as sharply as possible formal systems with 'living mathematics', he was not careful in his choice of words. He never repeated these statements.

However that may be, an episode that occurred shortly after the second World War led Brouwer again to speak his mind on the issue of psychologism (without mentioning his 1911 argument!), and this time in a more convincing manner. It is possible that the untenability of psychologism once again impressed itself on Brouwer when he realized, around 1927, that it does not go together well with the creating subject arguments that he then began to employ (see ch.5).

This episode started in 1946 with a paper by his former student Griss, who, as we saw in chapter 2, objected to the use of negation in intuitionistic mathematics, on the ground that it requires intuitions that we cannot have. In our discussion, the reply was to say that propositions express intentions, and that certain consequences of a proposition can be read of just from its intentional content. This reply is in line with other things Brouwer says, but he saw a possibility to be sharper, by exhibiting an example of a property that is necessarily negative (meaning that it cannot be written without a negation sign in front). Brouwer published this example in 1948, in the paper 'Essentially negative properties' [30]. It contains a weak counterexample to

$$\forall x \in \mathbb{R}(x \neq 0 \rightarrow x \# 0)$$

where $a \# b$ is the apartness relation defined as $\exists n(|a - b| > 2^{-n})$. A version of his argument we saw in chapter 5. It certainly shows that apartness is a stronger notion than inequality. According to Brouwer, it also shows that we know a negative property of α that cannot be written positively, so that, against Griss' contention, negation is an intuitionistically acceptable notion. This part of Brouwer's argument, however, is inconclusive: although it does show that the most obvious candidate for a positive equivalent fails, it does not show that there can be no such equivalent. But as we will see in a moment, the fact that Brouwer's proof establishes a weaker result than he thought is actually irrelevant for what it led him to say about psychologism.

In 1949, the Dutch mathematician and philosopher van Dantzig came to Griss's defence and published 'Comments on Brouwer's Theorem on Essentially-negative predicates' [47]. He argued that it is not clear what, in Brouwer's paper, is denoted by the term 'creating subject', and offers the following alternatives: the author himself, an arbitrary human individual, a human individual possessing some (which?) qualification, an 'infinite' sequence of such individuals, successively performing the activities, ascribed to the creating subject, or, finally, a more or less definite group of human individuals, for example, all mathematicians possessing some definite qualification. Van Dantzig's rejoinder to Brouwer is that the choice sequence $\alpha_1, \alpha_2, \alpha_3, \ldots$ may come to a stop and leave α undetermined, thus not constructing a real number at all. After all, the creating subject may have died before having decided p, or may have lost interest in the proposition p and therefore never decide it, or, if the creating subject is interpreted as a group, the group may lack unanimity; and van Dantzig adds that in any case, 'all these interpretations imply a semi-empirical thesis, viz. that there will "always" be a human being, willing and able to [decide p]'.

Note that all the interpretations of the creating subject that van Dantzig offers are psychological subjects. Brouwer studied the paper and on August 24, 1949, wrote the following letter in reply:[40]

> Many thanks for sending me the first copy of your 'Comments'. I am glad to see that these developments make the essentially negative properties meaningful also to those who do not recognize the

intuitionistic 'creating subject', because with respect to mathematics they hold the psychologistic point of view, or in any case insist on a 'plurality of mind'.[41]

As I told you already in conversation, my example is so much less vulnerable in principled intuitionism than in other positions, because although the intuitionistic creating subject can in advance pose restrictions (or forbid restrictions) on a given growing mathematical entity that is its creation, it cannot do so on its own possibilities to create.

If anything, your comments have strengthened my belief that psychologistic interpretations of intuitionistic mathematics, however interesting, can never be adequate.

Note that van Dantzig's argument is not concerned with negative properties as such, but with a general technique that Brouwer employs to exhibit one. This technique is of course the use of the creating subject in the definition of a real number, as we discussed in the previous chapter. In particular the 'solipsistic' aspect that all mathematics is done by this creating subject. This aspect implies that any mathematical proposition holds exactly if it has been established at some stage of the subject's activity.[42]

Van Dantzig's argument hinges on the implication: if the creating subject is a psychological subject, then Brouwer's example does not work. Brouwer accepts this implication. However, each construes the force of it differently. Van Dantzig starts from a psychologistic conception of the creating subject, and combines this with his implication by way of modus ponens. His conclusion is that Brouwer's example cannot work. Brouwer, on the other hand, insists that his example is a valid piece of intuitionistic mathematics and applies modus tollens, concluding that the creating subject should not be interpreted psychologistically. As they say, 'One man's modus ponens is another man's modus tollens'.

6.3 The creating subject as phenomenology's transcendental subject

As noted at the beginning of this cahpter, it has been suggested before that the creating subject is a transcendental subject. The Kantian construal of that notion has been the most popular; it seems only Roberts proposed the transcendental subject as it figures in Husserl's phenomenology. Let me explain the latter option first.

Whatever I experience as objectively existing, whether concrete or abstract, the acts in which this happens are always my acts. Husserl was struck by the fact that our experiences are before anything else subjective. Objectivities may be grasped, but this always happens in subjective acts. The question then is how subjectivity becomes aware of objects that transcend it. Husserl calls this 'the transcendental question'. Now, Husserl says that the subject meant in this question cannot be the pyschological. Why not? And what is the alternative to a psychological understanding? Husserl answers these questions by introducing his notion of the transcendental subject, for example in the following way.[43]

One realizes, Husserl says, that every positive or objective ontology leaves the relation with subjectivity unthematized. It does not speak of the experiencing, thinking, researching consciousness which apprehends these objects as such [82, p.27]. In this sense, such an ontology remains one-sided.

This subjectivity should not be construed as itself objective or part of a positive ontology; doing so would be to unthematize the relation between the subjective and the objective again. This means that consciousness of objects cannot be explained by introducing more objects to your philosophy. As the philosophical task is to elucidate how the subject becomes conscious of the objective, it would be a petitio to answer this by invoking knowledge that itself refers to something that exists objectively. Husserl calls this petitio 'the transcendental circle'. (One is reminded of Wittgenstein, Tractatus 5.632, 'The subject does not belong to the world, but is a limit to it'.)

It is seen that thematizing the relation between the subjective and the objective requires a radical reflection which focuses on how the objective is intentionally implied in the subjective.

Whereas the psychological subject is part of an objective world, the transcendental subject has or intends a world. Through its acts, the transcendental subject constitutes a world, and the subject thus *lets* the world manifest itself. A world without subjectivity, and many varieties of reductionism try to present it just like that, would be a world without meaning. But we do not merely act and react, we do not merely *do* things; we have cognitions, grasp truths, live in a space of reasons. This is possible because of the transcendental dimension to subjectivity. The transcendental subject, and now I will quote Stanley Cavell out of context, 'is responsible for everything that happens in its work—and not just in the sense that it is done, but in the sense that it is meant'.[44]

Note that the transcendental subject is not independent from the empirical subject that seems, in a phenomenologically precise sense, more natural to us. They are not two separate entities, but rather two different aspects of our subjectivity as a whole.

Husserl's conception of the transcendental subject is congenial to intuitionism. According to Husserl, there is an awareness of time at the transcendental level. This is of course not the time you can see on clocks—that is physical time, hence in the world. Rather, the time awareness consists in the awareness present in every intentional act, that other acts have preceded it and that others will follow it. In that sense, Husserl says, the transcendental subject never dies, because its acts always point to an open future [84, p.377ff]. He also calls it an 'eternally becoming Being' (p.381). This notion of time and the freedom implied by an always open future coincide exactly with the time that Brouwer's subject bases mathematics on. It also addresses van Dantzig's worry that maybe the subject's life comes to an end. Such a worry is valid for an empirical subject, but not for a transcendental one. A psychological or empirical subject will at some point have no future. On the other hand, a transcendental subject always has an open future, as a matter of essence. Thus, the creating subject could well be identified with phenomenology's transcendental subject considered in its essence.

How suitable, on the other hand, is a Kantian interpretation of the transcendental subject for the purposes of saving intuitionism from lapsing into a psychologism?

The transcendental subject or ego, for Kant, is the source of the pure categories. As such, it is the ground for all meaning and knowledge. He also claims that we cannot have *knowledge* of the transcendental ego, as it cannot be given to us in intuition. Here we have to take intuition in Kant's sense, of course, according to which intuition is always either of an empirical object or of one of the pure forms (contributed by our mind) through which empirical objects are given to us, space and time. The transcendental ego precisely makes intuition possible. However, we can, according to Kant, deduce the properties of this ego by considering what it must be like if experience as we have it is to be possible. Kant's analysis of the transcendental ego thus takes the form of a regressive analysis, of which the ideal result is a number of conditions. These are the conditions of possibility to have the experiences we have.

Kant based arithmetic on the intuition of time.[45] Brouwer took this from Kant and acknowledges it in his dissertation.[46] Mathematics is an example of synthetic a priori knowledge.[47] However, it consists in knowledge of possible objects, where by objects Kant means empirical objects. Mathematics describes the forms in time and space in which empirical objects can be given to us in our experience; this refers to arithmetic and geometry, respectively. In the second edition of the Transcendental Deduction, Kant stresses that the existence of empirical objects is a necessary condition for the possibility of mathematical knowledge:

> Mathematical concepts are not, therefore, by themselves knowledge, except on the supposition that there are things which allow of being presented to us only in accordance with the form of that pure sensible intuition. [91, B147]

Kant is not saying that mathematical propositions are empirical propositions. What he does say is that mathematical propositions are only possible in so far as there exists an empirical domain to which the mathematical concepts are applicable. As Arthur Collins puts it,

> Although Kant speaks of pure space and time as providing *a priori* objects for mathematics, the understanding explained here considerably deflates the ontological standing of pure objects ... He does not intend [mathematics] to be taken as a subject matter in itself, complete with its own inner objects. Mathematics is knowledge of possible empirical objects. [41, p.68]

There are several reasons to object to Kant's point of view from Brouwer's perspective.

First, unlike Kant, Brouwer thinks that mathematics does have an independent domain of objects. In a note to his Cambridge lectures, he writes that

'The stock of mathematical entities is a real thing, for each person, and for humanity' [37, p.90]. Incidentally, this note also shows Brouwer's belief in the intersubjectivity of intuitionistic mathematics. Moreover, in the genetic order of constitution described by Brouwer in 1948 [29], these mathematical entities are prior to empirical objects. Husserl shares the idea that mathematical objects form a domain of their own. Both hold that mathematics does not need a context of possible empirical objects to make sense. Kant's idea that it does they would reject as a kind of naturalism (in its insistence that the mathematical is dependent on, and limited by, some aspect of the empirical).

The further reasons actually are some of Husserl's criticisms of Kant. They have been commented on in the literature (the most important source is still Kern [94]); I mention them because I believe Brouwer would have had reason to share them.

The second reason is that Kant's account of the transcendental subject still presupposes objectivity [85, § 100]. His conception of knowledge is such that knowledge is marked by certainty of the type logic shows; combining this with the idea that the transcendental subject is the ground of all knowledge, he concludes that the transcendental subject is in some way like logical objects ('purely intellectual' [91, B423]).[48] However, Kant takes logic simply as a given, and does not inquire how logic itself is grounded in the transcendental ego. Kant should have added another question to his famous list, namely, 'How is pure logic possible?' As Husserl comments,

> Accordingly the transcendental problem that objective logic (no matter how broadly or narrowly) must raise concerning its field of ideal objectivities takes a position parallel to the transcendental problems of the sciences of realities. [85, p.264]

According to Brouwer, to find the deepest level of consciousness, we have to abandon logic [12, 29]. Like Husserl but unlike Kant, Brouwer recognizes that logic, too, is an accomplishment of the subject.

The third reason is that in his determination of the transcendental ego, Kant proceeds deductively. Even though this is not a *logical* deduction but a *transcendental* deduction, it does not consist in an analysis of what is *given* to us. However, Brouwer shared with Husserl the idea that existence and givenness are correlates of one another. 'There are no non-experienced truths' [29, p.1243]. Transcendental deduction is as alien to Brouwer as it is to Husserl. Of this procedure, Husserl says that Kant

> does get involved in his own sort of mythical talk, whose literal meaning points to something subjective, but a mode of the subjective which we are in principle unable to make intuitive to ourselves, whether through factual examples or through genuine analogy. [81, p.114]

For Husserl, to say that something exists is equivalent to saying that this thing can ideally be present to consciousness with full evidence. He thus strives to obtain evidence of the transcendental subject, not deductions of it. The transcendental subject is not a pure thought but is lived (this is exactly what Kant denies [91, B277]). As a method to obtain evidence for the transcendental subject, Husserl introduces a radical reflection called the transcendental reduction. One of Husserl's ways to the transcendental reduction I just described. Kant held that experience is always experience of empirical objects. Husserl disagreed and said that Kant's lack of the transcendental reduction is responsible for his overlooking a deeper layer of subjectivity than the empirical.

This brings us to the fourth reason. Kant's transcendental subject is a mundane subject—it is located in an objective world. However, according to Husserl, such an objective world can only be understood as constituted by the transcendental subject, which therefore must be non-mundane; otherwise that subject would be trapped in the transcendental circle. Indeed, Husserl claims (e.g., [81, § 31] this is what happens in Kant.[49] Brouwer, like Husserl, escapes this circle by recognizing a level of subjectivity that precedes the objective or empirical. For example, Brouwer describes a hierarchy of constitution processes, consisting of 'phases that consciousness has to pass through in its transition from its deepest home to the exterior world'. The subject cannot be identified with a psychological subject in the world; as Brouwer puts it, 'the home body of the subject'—after all, a part of the exterior world—is 'completely estranged from the subject'; calling psychological subjects 'object individuals', he adds that 'acts of the subject and acts of object individuals' are 'totally different phenomena' [29, pp.1235,1239].

My proposal, therefore, is that we identify intuitionism's creating subject not with Kant's, but with Husserl's transcendental subject, as far as mathematics is concerned. Doing so promises to solve the problem of how to account for intersubjectivity and points to a deeper analysis of other aspects of Brouwer's philosophy as well. It makes the descriptive richness of transcendental phenomenology available to the interpreter of Brouwer.[50]

Earlier, we saw that for Frege, the subjective is that which is different for different persons.[51] Let me repeat part of his quote:

> If we could grasp nothing but what is in ourselves, then a [genuine] conflict of opinions, [as well as] a reciprocity of understanding, would be impossible, since there would be no common ground, and no idea in the psychological sense can be such a ground.

For Frege, 'what is in ourselves', i.e., the subjective, is exhausted by the psychological. But in the notion of a transcendental subject are implied aspects of subjectivity that are the same for everyone precisely in virtue of each being a subject, and that in no way depend on the empirical. If mathematics can be founded on some of these aspects, then an account of intersubjectivity is within reach. If we construe the creating subject this way, then intersubjectivity is not a problem for, but rather a consequence of, the notion of the creating subject. While mathematics is ultimately traced back to subjectivity, this happens in a way that is necessarily the same for every subject, as mathematics then only depends on aspects that all subjects share simply because they are *subjects*. ('Intuitionistic mathematics is inner architecture' [29, p.1249].)

It is in this consideration that one finds a reply to worries that intuitionism might fall prey to a private language argument. Wittgenstein's argument aims to refute the idea that words could refer to something that cannot be known by anyone but the particular subject speaking. However, if the constructions in intuitionism are understood as constructions of the transcendental subject, then the private language argument doesn't apply to begin with [116, p.92]. For what is transcendental is eo ipso open to all subjects. The intuitionist's constructions, while carried out in his mind, are not epistemically private items.[52]

The reasoning towards a mathematics shared by a community of subjects proceeds from consideration on the single subject. As Husserl writes,

> In these meditations I carry out all constructions of knowledge and, in a certain manner, [all] practical [constructions] in a solipsistic attitude. At first I have no occasion to speak of an intersubjective thought, of intersubjective confirmation and truth ... But as soon as community is drawn into consideration ... then we fix, with an additional consideration, the observation that monosubjective mathematics is *eo ipso* intersubjective and, conversely, no intersubjective mathematics is possible that is not already completely grounded as monosubjective. [141, p.241][53]

There is a step to be explained here. For intersubjectivity, it is not enough that mathematics should happen to be the same for all subjects; they should also have a means to share this knowledge with one another [85, p.195,p.349]. How monosubjective mathematics, in a community of transcendental subjects, becomes intersubjective, that is, a common mathematics, depends on the introduction of a language for mathematics. This process has been outlined by Husserl in the essay that has become known under the title 'On the origins of geometry' [81, appendix VI]. Language, then, is not essential to mathematical activity as such, but it is a necessary tool to suggest mathematical constructions to others, and to recognize that two mathematicians share an intention. This is exactly Brouwer's view on the role of language in mathematics [11, p.169], [32, p.41].

These considerations may serve as an explanation of Kolmogorov's statement:

> The fact that *I* have solved a problem is a purely subjective fact that in itself has as yet no general interest. However, the logical and mathematical problems possess the special property *of the general validity of their solutions*: If I have solved a logical or a mathematical problem, then I can present this solution in a way that is intelligible to all and it is *necessary* that it be recognized as a correct solution although this necessity has to a certain extent an ideal character, for it presupposes a sufficient intelligence on the part of the listener. [97, p.330, original emphasis]

6.4 Further exploration

There is a further consideration that supports the transcendental interpretation of intuitionism, and in such a way that it ties intuitionism closer to Husserl than to Kant. Both Oskar Becker—one of Husserl's students—and Arend Heyting—one of Brouwer's—noted early on that intuitionistic logic can be interpreted in terms of intentions and their fulfilment. But they may not have guessed how close the relation between intentionality and intuitionism actually is. Let me illustrate this by discussing some paragraphs at the beginning of Brouwer's 'Consciousness, Philosophy, and Mathematics' from 1948 [29].[54]

> First of all an account should be rendered of the phases consciousness has to pass through in its transition from its deepest home to the exterior world in which we cooperate and seek mutual understanding ...
>
> *Consciousness* in its deepest home seems to oscillate slowly, willlessly, and reversibly between stillness and sensation. And it seems that only the status of sensation allows the initial phenomenon of the said transition. This initial phenomenon is a *move of time*. By a move of time a present sensation gives way to another present sensation in such a way that consciousness retains the former one as a past sensation, and moreover, through this distinction between present and past, recedes from both and from stillness, and becomes *mind*.
>
> As mind it takes the function of a subject experiencing the present as well as the past sensation as object. And by reiteration of this two-ity phenomenon, the object can extend to a world of sensations of motley plurality.
>
> In measure of the irreversibility with which the subject has receded from an element of the object, this element loses its egoicity, i.e. gets estranged from the subject, and in measure of this estrangement, mind becomes disposed to desire and apprehension, and consequently to positive or negative conative activity with respect to the element in question.

In this quote we find the idea of intentionality, the central role of time, and a level of consciousness ('its deepest home') at which time itself is constituted. It agrees with Husserl who says that 'Subjective time becomes constituted in the absolute timeless consciousness, which is not an object' [83, p.117] (for Kant, temporalization is a hidden function [91, B152-3]). This is immediately related to one of Husserl's deepest insights on intentionality and time, which one also finds here in Brouwer: the idea that it is the flow of time that makes possible the subject-object relation. As Brouwer says, the subject-object distinction is introduced into consciousness *through the distinction between present and past*. In an essay on intersubjectivity and the constitution of time in Husserl, James Mensch comments

> *Objekt* in German is *Gegenstand*. It is that which *stands against* the
> subject. This 'againstness' indicates a certain nonidentity, a certain
> distance, between the subject and its object. In transcending tempo-
> ral positions, the now of my actively constituting subject constantly
> opens up a *temporal distance* between itself and the constituted po-
> sitions ... In this, it also opens up the original distance between itself
> and its objects which are positioned in definite stretches of succes-
> sive time. All objectification involves such positioning in successive
> time. [original emphasis] [109, p.62]

For Husserl, then, objective consciousness presupposes consciousness of subjective time. For Kant, the relation is the reverse: subjective time consciousness
presupposes objective consciousness.[55] From what we have just seen in the
fragment from Brouwer, it is clear that his position on this is that of Husserl.

I have been arguing for a Husserlian reading of intuitionism from a conceptual point of view. Given that Husserl and Brouwer were contemporaries,
let me briefly consider the historical question whether Brouwer could have had
Husserl's transcendental subject in mind. Brouwer and Husserl met once, in
Amsterdam in 1928. They had long and interesting conversations. We know,
because Husserl says so in a letter to Heidegger of May 5 of that year [89]. What
we do not know, unfortunately, is what the subjects of their conversation were.
No records have been left. They also planned that Brouwer, who often traveled
in Germany, would visit Husserl soon (letter of Husserl's wife to Ingarden, May
6/9 1928 [89, p.239]); as far as we know, this never actually happened.

In Brouwer's thesis from 1907 [11], the main philosophical influence is Kant.
Brouwer was explicit about this. It is unlikely that Brouwer was aware of any
of Husserl's work then. (Incidentally, this was just the time when Husserl was
taking his transcendental turn; the first publication on this were his Ideen from
1913 [87].) Does this mean that, if my intended interpretation of Brouwer is
to have any historical plausibility, I am required to indicate a moment when
Brouwer shifted from a Kantian to a Husserlian type of view? No. Although,
as I have just said, the main influence on Brouwer was Kant, this influence was
limited to a very specific idea, namely, the idea to base mathematics on the
intuition of time. The other philosophical ideas that Brouwer had developed by
then were rather unlike anything one finds in Kant. They have rather different
views on causality, the possibility of Dinge an sich, the a priori intuition of
space, and ethics. It cannot be said, therefore, that Brouwer ever held Kantian
views in a broader sense.[56] Moreover, Kant is seldom referred to in Brouwer's
writings after his inaugural address from 1912 [15]. (A late mentioning is in
the second Vienna lecture [25].) It seems that, when Brouwer had consolidated
his views and had begun to make a reputation of his own, he no longer needed
Kant as an indication to the reader of the direction in which his thoughts were
developing.[57] The question why Brouwer on the one hand did mention Kant
in his early work, but, on the other hand, never alludes to Husserl in his later
work, remains.

Before closing, I had better note what seems to be a limitation to, or a need for qualification of, my proposal. Namely, it is not obvious that phenomenology (in mathematics) should be identified with intuitionism. Oskar Becker did make this identification by interpreting the phenomenological notion of constitution as the intuitionistic notion of construction. But Becker was perhaps unnecessarily restricting Husserl's notion here [103, p.194n.15]. As an indication of the implausibility of this identification, note that among the motives that led Husserl to develop phenomenology was the desire to devise a philosophical account of *classical* mathematics; likewise, when around 1959 Gödel turned to phenomenology, it was to find a justification of his *realism* in mathematics [63].

One way to negotiate this limitation is to suggest that the phenomenological considerations I have mentioned so far, while perhaps able to supply intuitionism as well as classical mathematics with a coherent interpretation, are too general to distinguish between the two. One way to differentiate them would be to distinguish levels of evidence and to say that intuitionism is the mathematics of a class of objects that are given to us with a particularly high degree of evidence. One can then extend the class of mathematical objects, at the cost of decreasing evidence of the objects one speaks about. This idea of levels of evidence has in fact been hinted at by Bernays [7], suggested by Heyting [74, p.103], and shared by Gödel and Wang [140, pp.214–217]

It should be added that it may be possible to find a phenomenological justification for objects that are admissible only in intuitionistic mathematics, such as choice sequences, which lead to results that are not classically valid. So it could be that, from a phenomenological point of view, the mathematical universe contains both typically classical and typically non-classical objects.

To conclude, I have argued that, on historical and conceptual grounds, the creating subject should be construed as a transcendental subject. Moreover, a Husserlian interpretation of the transcendental subject will serve Brouwer better than a Kantian. Finally, this construal shows that intuitionism is not psychologism and can account for intersubjectivity. That leaves us a mathematics in which we *do* know what we are talking about and that what we are saying is the shared truth.

Endnotes

[1] As it happens, there is an intuitionistic construction for such a and b, using an intuitionistically acceptable, deep theorem established by Gelfand that implies that $\sqrt{2}^{\sqrt{2}}$ is irrational.

[2] 'het scheppend subject' [28]; often translated as 'creative subject'. Van Dalen [42, p.394] has pointed out that 'creating' is more appropriate.

[3] The English translation by Heyting has 'are not' instead of 'were not'. To use 'are' might suggest that the 'new relations' are not intuitively given. Although Brouwer's original choice of words in Dutch does not contain a verb at all, it is clear from the whole passage that the exploration is not a linguistic affair, so that the transition is from one immediately perceived structure to the next (as opposed to a deductive step from one logical formula to the next); this speaks in favour of 'were not'.

[4] For a recent view on the role of language and logic in mathematics with striking parallels to Brouwer's as discussed in this section and the next, see [135].

[5] Detailed arguments along these lines have been developed by Gödel [62].

[6] This connection between Brouwer and Ryle was made by Wim Veldman [137].

[7] To Kreisel we owe the acute observation that 'It is an illusion—surely, not willful deception—to present studies on natural languages as pioneer work, to which correspondingly lax standards are to be applied. This simply overlooks the fact that, realistically speaking, such subjects as intuitionistic logic are also studies of natural languages, and their level of sophistication provides more appropriate standards.' [101, p.94]

[8] There is another sense in which different logics are possible, namely, according to what conditions one puts on the construction processes they describe: e.g. constructions on finite domains, or constructions given limited resources. In the text, logic without any such conditions is meant.

[9] Without giving due credit, to Brouwer's displeasure [23, p.42].

[10] These arguments evoke Frege's criticism of formalism in Grundlagen, §§96–99; there is, for better or for worse, no evidence that Brouwer ever read Frege.

[11] Brouwer to Morse, January 4, 1955. A copy of the letter is in the Brouwer Archive, Dept. of Philosophy, Utrecht University. The Archive holds the copyright.

[12] In fact there are different objects that can be founded on such an episode, depending on which of the episode's aspects one chooses to abstract from. The Swedish philosopher Sundholm has carefully discussed the various possibilities [129].

[13] Barzin and Errera defended the interpretation of intuitionistic logic as a three-valued logic, and valid refutations did not suffice to withold them from continuing to do so. This led to a famous debate. For a discussion and further references, see [68, section 5.4] and [104, pp.275–285].)

[14] 'Explanation' would be more appropriate, as Sundholm [128, p.159] has argued.

[15] Heyting to Becker July 23, 1933, printed in [133].

[16] This is Kolmogorov's diagnosis [96].

[17] If one leaves out axiom 10 of Heyting's system as, put anachronistically, was Kolmogorov's suggestion, adopted by Johansson (1936), one obtains the 'minimal calculus' or 'minimal logic'.

[18] Two decades later, Brouwer briefly considered the possibility of absolutely undecidable propositions [24, p.51], as, at the same time, did Heyting [72, p.308], [73, p.60]. However, both seem to have dropped the idea. I do not know if Heyting knew Brouwer's argument, but Heyting never gives it. It was rediscovered by Per Martin-Löf [106].

[19] Goldbach himself counted 1 among the primes, which is no longer customary; but if one does, then the condition 'greater than or equal to 4' can be dropped.

[20] A sequence $a(n)$ of rational numbers is called a Cauchy sequence exactly if for every rational number $\epsilon > 0$ there is a natural number N such that $|a_j - a_k| < \epsilon$ for all $j,k > N$. In words: the terms of the sequence eventually become arbitrarily close to one another.

[21] See http://www.informatik.uni-giessen.de/staff/richstein/ca/Goldbach.html

[22] Brouwer and Heyting liked to use the problem of whether the sequence 0123456789 occurs in the decimal expansion of π. That it does has now been proved, see http://www.cecm.sfu.ca/personal/jborwein/brouwer.html

[23] As pairs of rational numbers are enumerable, i.e., one can devise a 1-1 correspondence between them and the natural numbers, there is in fact no essential difference between choosing pairs of rationals or choosing natural numbers.

[24] Bishop [9, p.6] makes a humorous remark: 'In Brouwer's case there seems to have been a nagging suspicion that unless he personally intervened to prevent it the continuum would turn out to be discrete'.

[25] This is confirmed by a note in the Brouwer Archive from around 1928, and may be taken to contradict a certain remark by Heyting [36, p.565].

[26] Continuity *principles* for choice sequences, such as WC-N, should not be confused with the continuity *theorems*, theorems in intuitionistic analysis which will be discussed in the next chapter.

[27] See the forthcoming [2] for a more elaborate discussion than can be given here.

[28] Others can be found in [38] (two versions: I, ch.5 and II, 2.1.4), [126, appendix 11], and [34].

[29] As for the translation of various terms into English, I will follow that in van Heijenoort, except that I translate 'Menge' by 'spread' instead of 'set'.

[30] Brouwer, writing in German, speaks of 'gedankliche Beweisführungen'. In chapter 6, I will argue that these should not be interpreted psychologically.

[31] F is the letter 'wau' or 'digamma', which disappeared from the Greek alphabet early on, although in classical times it remained in use as the numeral for 6.

[32] Following the van Heijenoort translation. Brouwer used 'conservative' in English [37, p.78].

[33] In fact, they prove the equivalence of the analysis to a form of bar induction called BI_M. It implies BI_D, and BI_D plus the continuity principle implies BI_M. See also [49, pp.63–64].

[34] Brouwer in 1927 uses a slightly different fan.

[35] Indeed, Veldman has shown that the continuity theorem can be proved from just the continuity principle, without the bar and fan theorems [138].

[36] Brouwer used the fan theorem instead, e.g. [21, footnote 10], but that is more difficult.

[37] The rest of the 1927 paper after the proof of the uniform continuity theorem (not included in van Heijenoort [67]) is dedicated to the search for a characterization of less than total domains of definition of functions—hence the title of the paper—such that the functions defined on them behave in relevant ways like classical functions that are total and discontinuous.

[38] Not Julius König, known for his work on the continuum problem, but his son Dénes.

[39] What has become known as Kant's transcendental psychology is an attempt at a nonempirical psychology that evades subjectivism. 'Psychologism' as defined in the text excludes this variety. See footnote 49 below.

[40] The letter, which has not been published before, is kept in the Brouwer Archive, Dept. of Philosophy, Utrecht University. The Archive holds the copyright. The translation from the Dutch is my own.

[41] The term 'plurality of mind' refers to a group of subjects that all have direct access to each others' minds [29, p.1239].

[42] Compare the quote from Husserl on 'monosubjective' mathematics, p.81 below.

[43] Husserl's three ways have been discussed by Iso Kern [93], [94, §18].

[44] In the book by Vicky Hearne where I found this quote, it is used to characterize greatness in horses [66, p.162].

[45] Incidentally, this means that mathematics is essentially languageless for Kant as well. Edgar [51, p.117] may have been the first to point this out this in print.

[46] Further on, I argue that what is the same for Brouwer and Kant is the *function* of the intuition of time (with respect to mathematics), not the way this intuition comes about.

[47] In this paragraph, I am indebted to Arthur Collins's discussion [41, pp.66–68]. See also the discussions of Kant's view of mathematical objects by Thompson [130, pp.338–339], Parsons [114, pp.134,138,147–149], and Friedman [54, p.101ff].

[48] Tito [131, pp.81–84] discusses this.

[49] Husserl speaks of the error of 'transcendental psychologism'. He also discerns in Kant a 'transcendental psychology'. The latter is an eidetic psychology. As such it is of course legitimate; but it would be a category mistake to found mathematics on it, as 'even transcendental psychology also is precisely psychology' [86, § 28 footnote ***] and therefore a kind of naturalism (§ 38) [123], [141, ch.10].

[50] An elaborate and sympathetic interpretation of Brouwer from a Kantian point of view has been published by Carl Posy [118]. He writes 'I propose a Kantian framework—derived not merely from Kant's philosophy of mathematics but from his deeper metaphysicical views. I say "propose" here advisedly. For while Brouwer acknowledged that his intuitionism had certain Kantian roots . . . , the fact is that the metaphysical elements of Kant's philosophy spelled out in [Posy's section 'A Kantian framework for Brouwer] do not occur explicitly in Brouwer's

writings. I shall argue, however, that if the context of the debate is extended to include these Kantian themes, the coherence and consistency of what Brouwer had to say becomes apparent.' [118, p.293]. Posy does not expressly address the issue of the transcendental subject, but his proposal seems to imply that he conceives of the creating subject as Kant's transcendental subject. Although I agree with much of what Posy says in his paper, it will be clear that I do not think that in the end his proposal should be adopted.

[51]'Verschieden für verschiedene Menschen'. For a discussion of Frege's understanding of the subjective, see Angelelli, [1, pp. 231–234]. He demonstrates that Frege is not very clear on this point, and also that Frege at times seems to construe the objectivity of numbers as their being 'in' transcendental subjectivity (p.234). Angelelli makes it clear that he himself understands transcendental subjectivity in the Kantian sense (see his footnote 20 on p.245). This option, I argue in the main text, is not open to Brouwer.

[52] The argument for intersubjectivity of mathematics based on the transcendental nature of the subject is, of course, open to Kant as well, who indeed seems to take it for granted. Kant does have things to say about the intersubjectivity of empirical judgements, e.g. in §18–19 of the Prolegomena [92]. His account there is structurally analogous to the one I ascribe to him concerning mathematics: an objective intuition is only possible if perceptions are synthesized according to rules determined by the categories; and the categories are the same for all of us. This theme is further discussed by Mensch [108, p.125ff], who also explains why Husserl has to look for a structurally different account of intersubjectivity in the empirical domain; compare Zahavi [144].

[53]The original is on p.344 in the German edition of [85], and not included in the English translation by Cairns.

[54]The same ideas are also in earlier papers by Brouwer [10, 11, 24, 26], and, although Brouwer's formulations improved over the years, there has hardly been any discontinuity in the development of his philosophical framework.

[55]Morrison [112] and Ricoeur [119, ch.2] discuss this particular difference between Kant and Husserl.

[56]The American philosopher Charles Parsons informed me that on his visit to Brouwer in 1965, he asked about influence from Kant. But in his reply Brouwer said little about it, developing ideas of his own instead.

[57]This suggestion I owe to Dirk van Dalen.

References

English translations of items [10]–[35] can be found in volume I of Brouwer's Collected Works [36], unless noted otherwise.

[1] I. Angelelli. *Studies on Gottlob Frege and traditional philosophy*. Reidel, Dordrecht, 1967.

[2] M. van Atten and D. van Dalen. Arguments for the continuity principle. *Bulletin of Symbolic Logic*, 8(3), 2002.

[3] M. van Atten, D. van Dalen, and R. Tieszen. Brouwer and Weyl: The phenomenology and mathematics of the intuitive continuum. *Philosophia Mathematica*, 10(3):203–226, 2002.

[4] M. van Atten and R. Tragesser. Mysticism and mathematics: Brouwer, Gödel, and the common core thesis. In W. Deppert and M. Rahnfeld, editors, *Ist Religion rational begründbar/Is there a rational foundation of religion?* Leipziger Universitätsverlag, Leipzig, forthcoming.

[5] O. Becker. Beiträge zur phänomenologischen Begründung der Geometrie und ihrer physikalischen Anwendungen. *Jahrbuch für Philosophie und phänomenologische Forschung*, VI:385–560, 1923.

[6] P. Benacerraf and H. Putnam, editors. *Philosophy of mathematics: selected readings. (2nd ed.)*. Cambridge University Press, Cambridge, 1983. First ed. 1964.

[7] P. Bernays. Sur le platonisme dans les mathématiques. *L'Enseignement mathématique*, 34, 1935. English translation in [6], pp.258–271.

[8] P. Bernays. Hilbert, David. In P. Edwards, editor, *The encyclopedia of philosophy (vol. 3)*. Macmillan, New York, 1967.

[9] E. Bishop. *Foundations of constructive analysis*. McGraw-Hill, New York, 1967.

[10] L.E.J. Brouwer. *Leven, kunst en mystiek*. J. Waltman Jr., Delft, 1905. Full English translation in [39].

[11] L.E.J. Brouwer. *Over de grondslagen der wiskunde*. PhD thesis, Universiteit van Amsterdam, 1907. Quoted from English translation in [36], pp.13–101, which has the original pagination in the margin.

[12] L.E.J. Brouwer. De onbetrouwbaarheid der logische principes. *Tijdschrift voor Wijsbegeerte*, 2:152–158, 1908.

[13] L.E.J. Brouwer. Die mögliche Mächtigkeiten. In *Atti IV Congr. Intern. Mat. Roma*, volume III, pages 569–571, 1908.

[14] L.E.J. Brouwer. G. Mannoury, Methodologisches und Philosophisches zur Elementarmathematik. *Nieuw Archief voor Wiskunde*, 9:199–201, 1911. Quoted from English translation in [36], pp.121–122.

[15] L.E.J. Brouwer. *Intuïtionisme en Formalisme*. Clausen, Amsterdam, 1912. English translation 'Intuitionism and formalism' in [6], pp.77–89.

[16] L.E.J. Brouwer. Begründung der Mengenlehre unabhängig vom logischen Satz vom ausgeschlossenen Dritten. Erster Teil, Allgemeine Mengenlehre. *KNAW Verhandelingen*, 5:1–43, 1918.

[17] L.E.J. Brouwer. Über die Bedeutung des Satzes vom ausgeschlossenen Dritten in der Mathematik, insbesondere in der Funktionentheorie. *Journal für die reine und angewandte Mathematik*, 154:1–7, 1923. Quoted from English translation in [67], pp.335–341.

[18] L.E.J. Brouwer. Bemerkungen zum Beweise der gleichmässigen Stetigkeit voller Funktionen. *KNAW Proceedings*, 27:644–646, 1924.

[19] L.E.J. Brouwer. Bewijs dat iedere volle functie gelijkmatig continu is. *KNAW verslagen*, 33:189–193, 1924. English translation in [104], pp.36–39.

[20] L.E.J. Brouwer. Zur Begründung der intuitionistischen Mathematik I. *Mathematische Annalen*, 93:244–257, 1925.

[21] L.E.J. Brouwer. Über Definitionsbereiche von Funktionen. *Mathematische Annalen*, 97:60–75, 1927. Quoted from English translation in [67], pp.457–463.

[22] L.E.J. Brouwer. Zur Begründung der intuitionistischen Mathematik III. *Mathematische Annalen*, 96:451–488, 1927.

[23] L.E.J. Brouwer. Intuitionistische Betrachtungen über den Formalismus. *KNAW Proceedings*, 31:374–379, 1928. English translation in [104], pp.40–44.

[24] L.E.J. Brouwer. Mathematik, Wissenschaft und Sprache. *Monatshefte für Mathematik und Physik*, 36:153–164, 1929. Quoted from English translation in [104], pp.45–53.

[25] L.E.J. Brouwer. *Die Struktur des Kontinuums*. Komitee zur Veranstaltung von Gastvorträgen ausländischer Gelehrter der exakten Wissenschaften, Wien, 1930. English translation in [104], pp.54–63.

[26] L.E.J. Brouwer. Willen, Weten, Spreken. *Euclides*, 9:177–193, 1933. Quoted from English translation in [36], pp.443–446.

[27] L.E.J. Brouwer. Synopsis of the signific movement in the Netherlands. *Synthese*, 5:201–208, 1946.

[28] L.E.J. Brouwer. Richtlijnen der intuïtionistische wiskunde. *Indagationes Mathematicae*, 9:197, 1947. Quoted from English translation in [36], p.477.

[29] L.E.J. Brouwer. Consciousness, philosophy and mathematics. *Proceedings of the 10th International Congress of Philosophy, Amsterdam 1948*, 3:1235–1249, 1948.

[30] L.E.J. Brouwer. Essentieel negatieve eigenschappen. *Indagationes Mathematicae*, 10:322–323, 1948. Quoted from English translation in [36], pp.478–479.

[31] L.E.J. Brouwer. De non-aequivalentie van de constructieve en de negatieve orderelatie in het continuum. *Indagationes Mathematicae*, 11:37–39, 1949. English translation in [36], pp.495–496.

[32] L.E.J. Brouwer. Historical background, principles and methods of intuitionism. *South African Journal of Science*, 49:139–146, 1952.

[33] L.E.J. Brouwer. Over accumulatiekernen van oneindige kernsoorten. *Indagationes Mathematicae*, 14:439–441, 1952. Quoted from English translation in [36], pp.516–518.

[34] L.E.J. Brouwer. Points and spaces. *Canadian journal of mathematics*, 6:1–17, 1954.

[35] L.E.J. Brouwer. The effect of intuitionism on classical algebra of logic. *Proceedings of the Royal Irish Academy*, 57:113–116, 1955.

[36] L.E.J. Brouwer. *Collected works I. Philosophy and Foundations of Mathematics* (ed. A. Heyting). North-Holland, Amsterdam, 1975.

[37] L.E.J. Brouwer. *Brouwer's Cambridge lectures on intuitionism*. Cambridge University Press, Cambridge, 1981.

[38] L.E.J. Brouwer. *Intuitionismus*. Bibliographisches Institut, Wissenschaftsverlag, Mannheim, 1992.

[39] L.E.J. Brouwer. Life, art and mysticism. *Notre Dame Journal of Formal Logic*, 37(3):389–429, 1996. Translated and introduced by Walter van Stigt [127].

[40] L.E.J. Brouwer, F. van Eeden, J. van Ginneken, and G. Mannoury. Signifische dialogen. *Synthese*, 2:168–174,261–268,316–324, 1937. Quoted from English translation in [36], pp.447–452.

[41] A. Collins. *Possible experience. Understanding Kant's Critique of Pure Reason*. University of California Press, Berkeley, 1999.

[42] D. van Dalen. *Mystic, geometer, and intuitionist. The life of L.E.J. Brouwer. 1: The dawning revolution*. Clarendon Press, Oxford, 1999.

[43] D. van Dalen. Brouwer and Fraenkel on intuitionism. *Bulletin of Symbolic Logic*, 6(3):284–310, 2000.

[44] D. van Dalen. Intuitionistic logic. In L. Goble, editor, *The Blackwell guide to philosophical logic*, pages 224–257. Blackwell, Oxford, 2001.

[45] D. van Dalen. *L.E.J. Brouwer 1881–1966. Een biografie. Het heldere licht van de wiskunde*. Bert Bakker, Amsterdam, 2001.

[46] D. van Dalen. *L.E.J. Brouwer en de grondslagen van de wiskunde*. Epsilon, Utrecht, 2001.

[47] D. van Dantzig. Comments on Brouwer's theorem on essentially-negative predicates. *Indagationes Mathematicae*, 11:347–355, 1949.

[48] M. Dummett. Critical notice. L.E.J. Brouwer: *Collected Works*. *Mind*, 89:605–616, 1980.

[49] M. Dummett. *Elements of intuitionism (2nd, rev. edition)*. Clarendon Press, Oxford, 2000.

[50] M. Dummett. Is time a continuum of instants? *Philosophy*, 75:497–515, 2000.

[51] W.J. Edgar. Is intuitionism *the* epistemically serious foundation for mathematics? *Philosophia Mathematica*, 10(2):113–133, 1973.

[52] M. Epple. Did Brouwer's intuitionistic analysis satisfy its own epistemological standards? In V.F. Hendricks et al., editor, *Proof Theory*, pages 153–178. Kluwer, Dordrecht, 2000.

[53] G. Frege. *The Frege reader* (ed. M. Beany). Blackwell, Oxford, 1997.

[54] M. Friedman. *Kant and the exact sciences*. Harvard University Press, Cambridge, MA, 1992.

[55] V. Glivenko. Sur la logique de M. Brouwer. *Académie Royale de Belgique, Bulletin de la classe des sciences*, 14:225–228, 1928.

[56] K. Gödel. *Collected Works. I. Publications 1929–1936* (ed. S. Feferman et al.). Oxford University Press, Oxford, 1986.

[57] K. Gödel. Zum intuitionistischen aussagenkalkül. In *Collected Works. I. Publications 1929–1936* (ed. S. Feferman et al.) [56], pages 222–225. With English translation.

[58] K. Gödel. Zur intuitionistischen arithmetik und zahlentheorie. In *Collected Works. I. Publications 1929–1936* (ed. S. Feferman et al.) [56], pages 286–295. With English translation.

[59] K. Gödel. *Collected Works. II. Publications 1938–1974* (ed. S. Feferman et al.). Oxford University Press, Oxford, 1990.

[60] K. Gödel. Some remarks on the undecidability results. In *Collected Works. II. Publications 1938–1974* (ed. S. Feferman et al.) [59], pages 305–306.

[61] K. Gödel. *Collected Works. III: unpublished essays and lectures*. (ed. S. Feferman et al.). Oxford University Press, Oxford, 1995.

[62] K. Gödel. Is mathematics syntax of language? (*1953/9-III and *1953/9-V). In *Collected Works. III: unpublished essays and lectures*. (ed. S. Feferman et al.) [61], pages 334–362.

[63] K. Gödel. The modern development of the foundations of mathematics in the light of philosophy (1961). In *Collected Works. III: unpublished essays and lectures*. (ed. S. Feferman et al.) [61], pages 374–387.

[64] K. Green. *Dummett. Philosophy of language*. Polity Press, Oxford, 2001.

[65] G.F.C. Griss. Negationless intuitionistic mathematics I. *Indagationes Mathematicae*, 8:675–681, 1946.

[66] V. Hearne. *Adam's task*. Knopf, New York, 1986.

[67] J. van Heijenoort, editor. *From Frege to Gödel: A sourcebook in mathematical logic, 1879–1931*. Harvard University Press, Cambridge, MA, 1967.

[68] D. Hesseling. *Gnomes in the fog. The reception of Brouwer's intuitionism in the 1920s*. PhD thesis, Utrecht University, 1999.

[69] A. Heyting. Die formalen Regeln der intuitionistischen Logik I. *Sitzungsberichte der Preussischen Akademie von Wissenschaften*, pages 42–56, 1930. English translation in [104], pp.311–327.

[70] A. Heyting. Die formalen Regeln der intuitionistischen Logik II. *Sitzungsberichte der Preussischen Akademie von Wissenschaften*, pages 57–71, 1930.

[71] A. Heyting. Die formalen Regeln der intuitionistischen Logik III. *Sitzungsberichte der Preussischen Akademie von Wissenschaften*, pages 158–169, 1930.

[72] A. Heyting. Sur la logique intuitionniste. *Académie Royale de Belgique, Bulletin de la classe des sciences*, 16:957–963, 1930. English translation in [104], pp.306–310.

[73] A. Heyting. Die intuitionistische Grundlegung der Mathematik. *Erkenntnis*, 2:106–115, 1931. Quoted from English translation in [6], pp.52–61.

[74] A. Heyting. Intuitionism in mathematics. In R. Klibansky, editor, *La philosophie au milieu du vingtième siècle*, volume 1, pages 101–115. La nuova Italia, Firenze, 1958.

[75] A. Heyting. *Intuitionism, an introduction (Third, revised edition)*. North-Holland, Amsterdam, 1971.

[76] A. Heyting. Intuitionistic views on the nature of mathematics. *Synthese*, 27:79–91, 1974.

[77] A. Heyting. History of the foundation of mathematics. *Nieuw Archief voor Wiskunde*, XXVI(3):1–21, 1978.

[78] D. Hilbert. Die Grundlagen der Mathematik. *Abhandlungen aus dem Mathematischen Seminar der Hamburgischen Universität*, 6:65–85, 1928. Quoted from English translation in [67], pp.464–479.

[79] J. Hintikka. Intuitionistic logic as epistemic logic. *Synthese*, 127(1–2):7–19, 2001.

[80] E. Husserl. *Ideen zu einer reinen Phänomenologie und phänomenologischen Philosophie. Drittes Buch*, volume V of *Husserliana*. Martinus Nijhoff, Den Haag, 1952. English translation *Ideas pertaining to a pure phenomenology and to a phenomenological philosophy. Third book* by T. Klein and W. Pohl, Martinus Nijhoff, Dordrecht, 1980.

[81] E. Husserl. *Die Krisis der europäischen Wissenschaften und die transzendentale Phänomenologie*, volume VI of *Husserliana*. Martinus Nijhoff, Den Haag, 1954. Quoted from English translation *The crisis of European sciences and transcendental phenomenology* by D. Carr, Northwestern University Press, Evanston IL, 1970.

[82] E. Husserl. *Erste Philosophie (1923/1924). Zweiter Teil: Theorie der phänomenologischen Reduktion*, volume VIII of *Husserliana*. Martinus Nijhoff, Den Haag, 1959.

[83] E. Husserl. *Zur Phänomenologie des inneren Zeitbewußtseins (1893-1917)*, volume X of *Husserliana*. Martinus Nijhoff, Den Haag, 1966. Quoted from English translation *On the phenomenology of the consciousness of internal time* by J.B. Brough, Kluwer, Dordrecht, 1991.

[84] E. Husserl. *Analysen zur passiven Synthesis (1918–1926)*, volume XI of *Husserliana*. Martinus Nijhoff, Den Haag, 1966. English translation *Analyses concerning passive and active synthesis* by A. J. Steinbock, Kluwer, Dordrecht, 2001.

[85] E. Husserl. *Formale und Transzendentale Logik*, volume XVII of *Husserliana*. Martinus Nijhoff, Den Haag, 1974. Quoted from English translation *Formal and transcendental logic* by D. Cairns, Martinus Nijhoff, The Hague, 1969.

[86] E. Husserl. *Logische Untersuchungen. Erster Band*, volume XVIII of *Husserliana*. Martinus Nijhoff, Den Haag, 1975. English translation in volume 1 of [90].

[87] E. Husserl. *Ideen zu einer reinen Phänomenologie und phänomenologischen Philosophie. Erstes Buch*, volume III/1 of *Husserliana*. Martinus Nijhoff, Den Haag, 1976. English translation *Ideas pertaining to a pure phenomenology and to a phenomenological philosophy. First book* by F. Kersten, Kluwer, Dordrecht, 1983.

[88] E. Husserl. *Logische Untersuchungen. Zweiter Band, 1. Teil*, volume XIX/1 of *Husserliana*. Martinus Nijhoff, Den Haag, 1984. English translation in volume 1 and 2 of [90].

[89] E. Husserl. *Briefwechsel*. Kluwer, Dordrecht, 1994. Volumes I–X.

[90] E. Husserl. *Logical investigations (2 vols.)* (trl. J. Findlay, ed. D. Moran). Routledge, London, 2001.

[91] I. Kant. *Immanuel Kant's Critique of pure reason* (trl. Norman Kemp Smith). St Martin's Press, New York, 1965.

[92] I. Kant. *Kant's Prolegomena to Any Future Metaphysics* (trl.,ed. Gary Hatfield). Cambridge University Press, Cambridge, 1997.

[93] I. Kern. Die drei Wege zur transzendental-phänomenologischen Reduktion in der Philosophie Husserls. *Tijdschrift voor filosofie*, 24:303–349, 1962. English translation in *Husserl. Expositions and appraisals*, eds. F. Elliston and P. McCormick, University of Notre Dame Press, Notre Dame, 1977.

[94] I. Kern. *Husserl und Kant*. Martinus Nijhoff, Den Haag, 1964.

[95] S.C. Kleene and R.E. Vesley. *The foundations of intuitionistic mathematics. Especially in relation to recursive functions*. North-Holland, Amsterdam, 1965.

[96] A.N. Kolmogorov. O principe tertium non datur. *Matematiceskij Sbornik*, 32:646–667, 1925. Quoted from English translation in [67], pp.416–437.

[97] A.N. Kolmogorov. Zur Deutung der intuitionistischen Logik. *Mathematische Zeitschrift*, 35:58–65, 1932. Quoted from English translation in [104], pp.328–334.

[98] S. Körner. *The philosophy of mathematics*. Hutchinson, London, 1960.

[99] G. Kreisel. Informal rigour and completeness proofs. In I. Lakatos, editor, *Problems in the philosophy of mathematics*, pages 138–186. North-Holland, Amsterdam, 1967.

[100] G. Kreisel. Church's thesis and the ideal of informal rigour. *Notre Dame Journal of Formal Logic*, 28(4):499–519, 1987.

[101] G. Kreisel. Gödel's excursions into intuitionistic logic. In P. Weingartner and L. Schmetterer, editors, *Gödel remembered*. Bibliopolis, Napoli, 1987.

[102] G.W. Leibniz. *Philosophical essays* (ed.,trl. R. Ariew and D. Garber). Hackett, Indianapolis, 1989.

[103] D. Lohmar. *Phänomenologie der Mathematik. Elemente einer phänomenologischen Aufklärung der mathematischen Erkenntnis nach Husserl*. Kluwer, Dordrecht, 1989.

[104] P. Mancosu. *From Brouwer to Hilbert. The debate on the foundations of mathematics in the 1920s*. Oxford University Press, Oxford, 1998.

[105] G. Mannoury. *Handboek der analytische significa. I: Geschiedenis en begripstechniek*. Kroonder, Bussum, 1947.

[106] P. Martin-Löf. Verificationism then and now. In W. DePauli-Schimanovich, E. Köhler, and F. Stadler, editors, *The foundational debate: complexity and constructivity in mathematics and physics*, pages 187–196. Kluwer, Dordrecht, 1995.

[107] E. Martino and P. Giaretta. Brouwer, Dummett, and the bar theorem. In *Atti del Congresso Nazionale di Logica, Montecatini Terme, 1–5 Ottobre 1979*, Napoli, 1981.

[108] J. Mensch. *Intersubjectivity and transcendental idealism*. State University of New York Press, Albany, NY, 1988.

[109] J. Mensch. *After modernity. Husserlian reflections on a philosophical tradition*, chapter Intersubjectivity and the constitution of time. State University of New York Press, Albany, NY, 1996.

[110] J.N. Mohanty. *Husserl and Frege*. Indiana University Press, Bloomington, IN, 1982.

[111] J.N. Mohanty. Psychologism. In M.A. Notturno, editor, *Perspectives on psychologism*, pages 1–9. Brill, Leiden, 1989.

[112] R. Morrison. Kant, Husserl and Heidegger on time and the unity of consciousness. *Philosophy and phenomeonlogical research*, 39:182–198, 1978.

[113] J. Myhill. Notes towards an axiomatization of intuitionistic analysis. *Logique et Analyse*, 35:280–297, 1967.

[114] C. Parsons. *Mathematics in philosophy*. Cornell University Press, Ithaca, NY, 1983.

[115] C. Parsons. Intuition in constructive mathematics. In J. Butterfield, editor, *Language, mind and logic*, pages 211–229. Cambridge University Press, Cambridge, 1986.

[116] T. Placek. *Mathematical intuitionism and intersubjectivity. A critical exposition of arguments for intuitionism*. Kluwer, Dordrecht, 1999.

[117] C. Posy. Mathematics as a transcendental science. In Seebohm et al. [124], pages 107–131.

[118] C. Posy. Brouwer versus Hilbert: 1907–1928. *Science in context*, 11(2):291–325, 1998.

[119] P. Ricoeur. *Temps et récit. III: Le temps raconté*. Seuil, Paris, 1985. English translation *Time and narrative (vol.3)* by K. Blamey and D. Pellauer, Chicago University Press, Chicago, 1990.

[120] J. Roberts. *The logic of reflection. German philosophy in the twentieth century*. Yale University Press, New Haven, 1992.

[121] S. Rosen. *The limits of analysis*. Basic Books, New York, 1980.

[122] G. Ryle. Thinking and self-teaching. In *On thinking*, pages 65–78. Blackwell, Oxford, 1979.

[123] T. Seebohm. Psychologism revisited. In Seebohm et al. [124], pages 149–182.

[124] T. Seebohm, D. Føllesdal, and J. Mohanty, editors. *Phenomenology and the formal sciences*. Kluwer, Dordrecht, 1991.

[125] W.P. van Stigt. L.E.J. Brouwer, the signific interlude. In A.S. Troelstra and D. van Dalen, editors, *The L.E.J. Brouwer centenary symposium*, pages 505–512, Amsterdam, 1982. North-Holland.

[126] W.P. van Stigt. *Brouwer's intuitionism*. North-Holland, Amsterdam, 1990.

[127] W.P. van Stigt. Introduction to *Life, Art and Mysticism*. *Notre Dame Journal of Formal Logic*, 37(3):381–387, 1996.

[128] G. Sundholm. Constructions, proofs and the meaning of logical constants. *Journal of philosophical logic*, 12:151–172, 1983.

[129] G. Sundholm. Questions of proof. *Manuscrito*, XVI(2):47–70, 1993.

[130] M. Thompson. Singular terms and intuitions in Kant's epistemology. *Review of metaphysics*, 26:314–343, 1972–1973.

[131] J.M. Tito. *Logic in the Husserlian context*. Northwestern University Press, Evanston, Illinois, 1990.

[132] A.S. Troelstra. *Principles of intuitionism*. Springer, Berlin, 1969.

[133] A.S. Troelstra. Arend Heyting and his contributions to intuitionism. *Nieuw Archief Voor Wiskunde*, 29:1–23, 1981.

[134] A.S. Troelstra and D. van Dalen. *Constructivism in Mathematics (2 vols.)*. North-Holland, Amsterdam, 1988.

[135] J. Väänänen. Second-order logic and foundations of mathematics. *Bulletin of Symbolic Logic*, 7(4):504–520, 2001.

[136] W. Veldman. An intuitionistic completeness theorem for intuitionistic predicate logic. Technical report, Mathematisch Instituut, Katholieke Universiteit Nijmegen, May 1974.

[137] W. Veldman. *Investigations in intuitionistic hierarchy theory*. PhD thesis, Catholic University of Nijmegen, 1981.

[138] W. Veldman. On the continuity of functions in intuitionistic real analysis. Some remarks on Brouwer's paper: "Ueber Definitionsbereiche von Funktionen". Technical report, Mathematisch Instituut, Katholieke Universiteit Nijmegen, April 1982.

[139] H. Wang. To and from philosophy—discussions with Gödel and Wittgenstein. *Synthese*, 88:229–277, 1991.

[140] H. Wang. *A logical journey. From Gödel to philosophy*. MIT Press, Cambridge, MA, 1996.

[141] D. Welton. *The other Husserl*. Indiana University Press, Bloomington, IN, 2001.

[142] H. Weyl. *Das Kontinuum. Kritische Untersuchungen über die Grundlagen der Analysis*. Veit, Leipzig, 1918. English translation *The continuum. A critical examination of the foundation of analysis*, trl. S. Pollard and T. Bole, Dover Publications, New York, 1994.

[143] L. Wittgenstein. *Ludwig Wittgenstein and the Vienna Circle. Conversations recorded by Friedrich Waismann* (ed. B. McGuinness). Blackwell, Oxford, 1979.

[144] D. Zahavi. *Husserl and transcendental intersubjectivity. A response to the linguistic-pragmatic critique*. Ohio University Press, Athens, OH, 2001.